I NEVER THOUGHT I'D SEE THE DAY!

CULTURE AT THE CROSSROADS

Dr. David Jeremiah

with Dr. David Jeremiah

CONTENTS

ABOUT
DR. DAVID JEREMIAH
AND TURNING POINT

D r. David Jeremiah is the founder of Turning Point, a ministry committed to providing Christians with sound Bible teaching relevant to today's changing times through radio and television broadcasts, audio series, books, and rallies. Dr. Jeremiah's common-sense teaching on topics such as family, prayer, worship, angels, and biblical prophecy forms the foundation of Turning Point.

David and his wife, Donna, reside in El Cajon, California, where he serves as the senior pastor of Shadow Mountain Community Church. David and Donna have four children and ten grandchildren.

In 1982, Dr. Jeremiah brought the same solid teaching to San Diego television that he shares weekly with his congregation. Shortly thereafter, Turning Point expanded its ministry to radio. Dr. Jeremiah's inspiring messages can now be heard worldwide on radio, television, and the Internet.

Because Dr. Jeremiah desires to know his listening audience, he travels nationwide holding ministry rallies and spiritual enrichment conferences that touch the hearts and lives of many people. According to Dr. Jeremiah, "At some point in time, everyone reaches a turning point; and for every person, that moment is unique, an experience to hold onto forever. There's so much changing in today's world that sometimes it's difficult to choose the right path. Turning Point offers people an understanding of God's Word as well as the opportunity to make a difference in their lives."

Dr. Jeremiah has authored numerous books, including *Escape the Coming Night* (Revelation), *The Handwriting on the Wall* (Daniel), *Overcoming Loneliness, Grand Parenting, The Joy of Encouragement, Prayer—The Great Adventure, God in You* (Holy Spirit), *Gifts from God* (Parenting), *Jesus' Final Warning, When Your World Falls Apart, Slaying the Giants in Your Life, My Heart's Desire, Sanctuary, Life Wide Open, Searching for Heaven on Earth, The Secret of the Light, Captured by Grace, Discover Paradise, Grace Givers, Why the Nativity?, Signs of Life, The 12 Ways of Christmas, 1 Minute a Day, What in the World Is Going On?,* and *The Coming Economic Armageddon.*

ABOUT THIS
STUDY GUIDE

T he purpose of this Turning Point study guide is to reinforce
Dr. David Jeremiah's dynamic, in-depth teaching and to aid the
reader in applying biblical truth to his or her daily life. This
study guide is designed to be used in conjunction with Dr. Jeremiah's
I Never Thought I'd See the Day! audio series, but it may also be used
by itself for personal or group study.

STRUCTURE OF THE LESSONS

Each lesson is based on one of the messages in the *I Never Thought
I'd See the Day!* compact disc series and focuses on specific passages in
the Bible. Each lesson is composed of the following elements:

• *Outline*

The outline at the beginning of the lesson gives a clear, concise
picture of the topic being studied and provides a helpful framework
for readers as they listen to Dr. Jeremiah's teaching.

• *Overview*

The overview summarizes Dr. Jeremiah's teaching on the passage
being studied in the lesson. Readers should refer to the Scripture
passages in their own Bibles as they study the overview. Unless
otherwise indicated, Scripture verses quoted are taken from the New
King James Version.

• *Application*

This section contains a variety of questions designed to help
readers dig deeper into the lesson and the Scriptures, and to apply
the lesson to their daily lives. For Bible study groups or Sunday
school classes, these questions will provide a springboard for group
discussion and interaction.

• *Did You Know?*

This section presents a fascinating fact, historical note, or insight
that adds a point of interest to the preceding lesson.

Using This Guide for Group Study

The lessons in this study guide are suitable for Sunday school classes, small-group studies, elective Bible studies, or home Bible study groups. Each person in the group should have his or her own study guide.

When possible, the study guide should be used with the corresponding compact disc series. You may wish to assign the study guide lesson as homework prior to the meeting of the group and then use the meeting time to listen to the CD and discuss the lesson.

For Continuing Study

For a complete listing of Dr. Jeremiah's materials for personal and group study call 1-800-947-1993, go online to www.DavidJeremiah.org, or write to: Turning Point, P.O. Box 3838, San Diego, CA 92163.

Dr. Jeremiah's *Turning Point* program is currently heard or viewed around the world on radio, television, and the Internet in English. *Momento Decisivo*, the Spanish translation of Dr. Jeremiah's messages, can be heard on radio in every Spanish speaking country in the world. The television broadcast is also broadcast by satellite throughout the Middle East with Arabic subtitles.

Contact Turning Point for radio and television program times and stations in your area. Or visit our website at www.DavidJeremiah.org

I NEVER THOUGHT I'D SEE THE DAY!
CULTURE AT THE CROSSROADS

Gordon E. Moore was a co-founder of Intel, the largest computer chip manufacturer in the world. In 1965 he published a scientific paper in which he observed that the number of components (transistors) in semiconductor circuit boards had doubled ever since the invention of integrated circuits in 1958. He predicted then that the trend would continue for at least a decade—a prophetic statement that has proven accurate well into the twenty-first century. For example, in 1971 engineers could fit 2,300 transistors on a circuit board; by 2010 the number had reached 2.6 billion. What became known as "Moore's Law" has guided planning in the computer industry for four decades.[1]

What does Moore's Law mean? Generally speaking, that computing power has doubled every year. The average laptop computer or smart phone now has more processing power than older room-size computers—and the processing power continues to grow exponentially.

Rapid changes in digital technology have become almost overwhelming in recent years. But the technology venue is only symptomatic of changes going on all around us—and not all changes have been for the good. Our world and our nation—and even our beloved Church—are changing in ways that I never thought I would see.

This study guide is based on my 2011 book, *I Never Thought I'd See the Day!* . . . . It is actually the fourth book I've written in as many years dealing with the changes happening around us. The economic tsunami of 2008 that started in the United States washed over the shores of the rest of the world. That event, and its ripple effects, has resulted in a heightened sense of insecurity; tried and true institutions and values have become fair game for the world's change-mongers. The "new normal" in our world is debt, economic instability, political upheaval throughout the Middle East, unemployment, declining standards of morality, new definitions of marriage and family, and theocratic militants on a mission from their god to destroy all who don't agree with them.

And that's just the world! Within Christendom the changes are happening as well. Jesus Christ is no longer honored as the world's most influential person in the nation that has historically honored Him the most. He is now the source of humor and the butt of jokes in the media, treated in a way that no other religious figure is treated. The Church itself is trying so hard to be relevant that she is making herself increasingly irrelevant. And the Bible—the book that informed the philosophies of the founding fathers as they shaped the world's most successful political experiment—has been shuffled further and further to the edges of meaningful cultural conversation. Many Christians enter and leave their churches on Sunday morning without any meaningful or life-changing exposure to the Word of God.

My previous three books[2] dealt with the present and the future, but *I Never Thought I'd See the Day* . . . looks at the present in light of the past—nine specific changes I never thought I would see in our world and in the church: the rise of angry atheists, intensifying of spiritual warfare, irrelevance of the church, marginalization of the Bible, profaning of Jesus Christ, redefinition of marriage, loss of America's moral compass, the rise of militant, rogue nations, and the erosion of America's loyalty to Israel.

The book, and this study guide, concludes with a chapter on what every Christian must do to stand firm in the midst of a world that is changing in ways I never thought I would see.

Notes:

1. "Moore's law," Wikipedia.com. http://en.wikipedia.org/wiki/Moore%27s_law accessed 6-8-11.

2. *What in the World Is Going On?* (2008), *Living with Confidence in a Chaotic World— What on Earth Should We Do Now?* (2009), and *The Coming Economic Armageddon —What Bible Prophecy Warns About the New Global Economy* (2010).

...WHEN ATHEISTS WOULD BE ANGRY

Selected Scriptures

In this lesson we explore what is making contemporary atheists so angry.

OUTLINE

There have always been atheists, and they have for the most part taken a passive posture in the culture. But in recent years, atheists have become angry and proactive—fighting back against a God in whom they profess not to believe! But there are ways to explain their new aggression.

I. **Atheists Are Angry Because Their Arrogance Is Diminishing Them**

II. **Atheists Are Angry Because Their Advocates Are Deserting Them**

III. **Atheists Are Angry Because Their Arguments Are Dividing Them**

IV. **Atheists Are Angry Because Their Adversaries Are Defeating Them**

V. **Atheists Are Angry Because Their Amnesia Is Discrediting Them**

VI. **Atheists Are Angry Because Their Assessments Are Deceiving Them**

On the same day that Rev. Jerry Falwell died in 2007, CNN's Anderson Cooper interviewed outspoken atheist Christopher Hitchens for his reaction to Falwell's life and death:

COOPER: I'm not sure you believe in heaven, but, if you do, do you think Jerry Falwell is in it?

HITCHENS: No, and I think it's a pity that there isn't a hell for him to go to.

COOPER: What is it about him that brings up such vitriol?

HITCHENS: The empty life of this ugly little charlatan proves only one thing, that you can get away with the most extraordinary offenses to morality and to truth in this country if you will just get yourself called reverend.

COOPER: Whether you agree or not with his reading of the Bible, you don't think he was sincere in what he spoke?

HITCHINS: No. I think he was a conscious charlatan and bully and fraud. And I think, if he read the Bible at all— and I would doubt that he could actually read any long book…that he did so only in the most hucksterish, as we say, Bible-pounding way.[1]

In his book, *The God Delusion*, leading British atheist Richard Dawkins spews out his anger at God in these words:

"The God of the Old Testament is arguably the most unpleasant character in all of fiction: jealous and proud of it, a petty, unjust, unforgiving control freak; a vindictive, bloodthirsty ethnic cleanser; a misogynistic, homophobic, racist, infanticidal, genocidal, filicidal, pestilential, megalomaniacal, sadomasochistic, capriciously malevolent bully."[2]

A group of atheist intellectuals has arisen in the last five or six years that is being called the "New Atheists." They have written a spate of new books bashing the idea of religion and defending an atheistic worldview. The irony of the angry tone exhibited by today's leading atheists is that they seem to be angry at someone they profess not to believe in! Is that rational? Is that a good defense for their position?

In this lesson we will examine six reasons for the anger of these modern "New Atheists."

ATHEISTS ARE ANGRY BECAUSE THEIR ARROGANCE IS DIMINISHING THEM

I believe one of the reasons atheists are angry is because their own actions are making them look small in the eyes of observers. Author Mary Eberstadt has said about the New Atheists,

> "Their movement has repeatedly assailed religious people as self-righteous, ignorant of history and humorless, all the while remaining self-righteous, ignorant of history, and humorless itself to a quite remarkable degree."[3]

Even the term the new atheists are using to describe themselves —the "brights"—is not helping their cause as it seems to suggest they think they are brighter than everyone else. But these observations by Stevel Waldman in a National Public Radio commentary suggest the idea may have backfired:

> "I'm not sure what the image buffers were aiming for, but the name 'The Brights' succinctly conveys the sense that this group thinks it's more intelligent than everyone else. The rest of us would be 'The Dims,' I suppose. Daniel C. Dennett wrote, in a recent *New York Times* op-ed, 'We Brights don't believe in ghosts, or elves, or the Easter Bunny, or God.'"[4]

Let's put aside the questionable intelligence of trying to improve your image by choosing a title that makes everyone hate you; they might as well have chosen 'The Smugs' or 'The Smartypants.' Let's instead, examine the substance of their platform. . . .

What about their bolder assertion, or implication, that people who believe in god [sic] or the supernatural are just not as, well, bright? In fact, two surveys earlier this year—one from Harris, and one from Gallup—indicate that even supernatural religious beliefs are held not only by most Americans, but by the majority of well-educated Americans.

Listen to these numbers "55 percent of people with post-graduate degrees (lawyers, doctors, dentists, and the like) believe in the devil. Fifty-three percent believe in hell. Seventy-two percent believe in miracles. Remember these are people with post-graduate educations. Seventy-eight percent of them believe in the survival of the soul after death. Sixty percent believe in the virgin birth. And sixty-four percent believe in the resurrection of Christ."[5]

One of the clear messages of the Bible is the danger of pride, the original sin. It finds its place on God's hate list in Proverbs 6:16.

And King Solomon warned that, "Pride goes before destruction, and a haughty spirit before a fall" (Proverbs 16:18). The arrogance of the New Atheists is demeaning them, not defending them.

ATHEISTS ARE ANGRY BECAUSE THEIR ADVOCATES ARE DESERTING THEM

A British scholar named Antony Flew set the agenda for modern atheism with a 1950 essay titled "Theology and Falsification." It was widely read and reprinted and became a core document in the atheism movement. Author of more than 30 books, he rocked the intellectual world with a 2007 book titled *There Is a God*.[5] In this book he professed to having made a commitment to go wherever the evidence led—and the evidence led him to accept the existence of a Creator God. This was quite a shock to fellow atheists— especially many of the New Atheists—who had looked at Flew as one of their standard bearers. An Associated Press story about Flew and his new book said, "A British philosophy professor who has been a leading champion of atheism for more than a half-century has changed his mind. He now believes in God."[6]

Flew is now deceased and as far as we know he never came to place his faith in the God of the Bible. But he did come to the scientific conclusion that atheism is not logically sustainable. The evidence says otherwise.

A. N. Wilson, once thought to be the next C. S. Lewis, rejected and then regained his faith after concluding that atheists "are missing out on some very basic experiences of life."[7] He found a parallel between Lewis's rejection of faith and then becoming a Christian and his own journey, and gradually realized Christians had better answers for the complexities of life than did atheists, that "the perception of his atheist friends seemed rather 'parochial and flat.'"[8] "Listening to Bach and reading the works of religious authors, he realized that their 'perception of life was deeper, wiser, and more rounded than my own.'"[9] So he turned from atheism back to God.

Matthew Parris is another well-known British atheist who, upon visiting Christian aid workers in Malawi and seeing lives transformed by the Gospel, wrote that it "confounds my ideological beliefs, stubbornly refuses to fit my worldview, and has embarrassed my growing belief that there is no God."[10] He hasn't turned to God yet, but there are obviously cracks in his atheistic foundation for life.

And then there is Peter Hitchens, brother of the New Atheist Christopher Hitchens whom I have already mentioned. Peter Hitchens was also an atheist, though not one of the outspoken New Atheists —notice I said "was." He has told the dramatic story of his return to faith in God in his book, *The Rage Against God*.[11] Years spent in the former Soviet Union as a journalist exposed him firsthand to the impact of national atheism on human beings, how political leaders lived in luxury while ignoring the terrible plight of the common Soviet citizen. He couldn't reconcile the supposed intellectual superiority of atheism with its practical, Darwinian results seen in the survival of the fittest in the Soviet Union. He rejected atheism and turned back to the Christian God of his upbringing.

Atheism is not the bulwark of belief that the New Atheists would have you believe it is. And they are not happy that some in their own ranks have deserted the fold.

ATHEISTS ARE ANGRY BECAUSE THEIR ARGUMENTS ARE DIVIDING THEM

A key argument of atheists is that religion is responsible for most of the evil and pain in the history of the world. In his book, *How the Mind Works*, Steven Pinker writes,

"Religions have given us stonings, witch-burnings, crusades, inquisitions, jihads, fatwas, suicide bombers, abortion clinic gunmen, and mothers who drown their sons so they can be happily reunited in heaven. As Blaise Pascal wrote, 'Men never do evil so completely and cheerfully as when they do it from religious conviction.'"[12]

First, let's agree with history: There have been terrible atrocities committed in the name of religion and, yes, in the name of Christ. But what has been done in the name of Christianity has been blown vastly out of proportion as scholar Dinesh D'Souza documents in his book, *What's So Great About Christianity*.[13] Focusing on three specific periods of history—the Crusades, the Spanish Inquisition, and the Salem Witch Trials—D'Souza gives us facts about the degree of suffering that actually occurred. That is not to justify what was done in those periods. But it is to put it in historical context and demonstrate how, compared to other similar atrocities—and compared to the good Christianity has accomplished—those three events are not grounds for the New Atheists' blanket condemnation of religion, Christianity in particular.

Atheists insist that Christianity must accept blame for the few who misapply its truths. This is no more logical than a professor being forced to assume blame for the few who fail his course compared to the many who pass with flying colors.[14]

ATHEISTS ARE ANGRY BECAUSE THEIR ADVERSARIES ARE DEFEATING THEM

In his book *There Is a God*,[15] Antony Flew tells about meeting an Israeli scientist named Gary Schroeder who refuted, to Flew's satisfaction, the "monkey theory" of creation. This theory is supposed to illustrate the chance that evolution could have happened and that creation doesn't necessitate the existence of God. The monkey theorem says that if you place a group of monkeys in a room with typewriters, they will eventually produce the equivalent of a Shakespearean sonnet—by banging randomly on the keyboards.

As ridiculous as that sounds, many atheistic evolutionists believe in the monkey theory; they believe it proves that chance evolution can account for creation. But, according to Flew, the theory was actually tested by the British National Council of Arts. They put a computer in a cage with six monkeys and after one month there was not one single word in the 50 pages of typed gibberish they produced; not even an "I" or an "a" with spaces on either side that could be interpreted as a word.

Learning of the failed test had a big impact on Antony Flew. It was another example of the failure of atheistic thinking to stand up when tested.

ATHEISTS ARE ANGRY BECAUSE THEIR AMNESIA IS DISCREDITING THEM

Richard Dawkins has written, "There is not the smallest evidence . . . that atheism systematically influences people to do bad things. Individual atheists may do evil things but they don't do evil things in the name of atheism."[16]

Really? Consider this research by Dinesh D'Souza:

"In the past hundred years or so, the most powerful atheist regimes—Communist Russia, Communist China, and Nazi Germany—have wiped out people in astronomical numbers. Stalin was responsible for around twenty million deaths . . . . Mao Zedong's (Chinese) regime a staggering seventy million deaths. . .Hitler comes in a distant third with around ten million murders, six million of them Jews . . .We have to realize that atheist regimes have in a single century murdered more than one hundred million people."[17]

Atheists have forgotten their world history! Tragedies that have occurred in the name of religion are miniscule compared to those done in the name of atheism. D'Souza continues:

> "Whatever the cause for why atheist regimes do what they do, the indisputable fact is that the religions of the world put together in three thousand years have not managed to kill anywhere near the number of people killed in the name of atheism in the past few decades. It's time to abandon the mindlessly repeated mantra that religious belief has been the main source of human conflict and violence. Atheism, not religion, is responsible for the worst mass murders in history."[18]

ATHEISTS ARE ANGRY BECAUSE THEIR ASSESSMENTS ARE DECEIVING THEM

Based on the best research, the number of atheists in the world is actually decreasing annually while the number of religious adherents is increasing:

> "[Atheists] numbers have actually dropped over the past decade, despite the caterwauling of Richard Dawkins, Christopher Hitchens, and Co. One cluster of comparative growth statistics is striking. As of mid-2011, there will be an average of 80,000 new Christians per day (of whom 31,000 will be Catholics) and 79,000 new Muslims per day, but *300 fewer atheists* every 24 hours."[19]

Oxford and King's College (London) scholar Alister McGrath summarizes it well:

> "Atheist thinkers are more than happy to appear on the nation's chat shows to promote their latest book. But they have failed to communicate a compelling vision of atheism that is capable of drawing and holding large numbers."[20]

It's no wonder that one of the world's most famous atheists, the late Bertrand Russell, said near the end of his life, "Nothing can penetrate the loneliness of the human heart except the highest intensity of the sort of love the religious teachers have preached."[21]

Thanks be to God that "the heavens declare the glory of God; and the firmament shows His handiwork!" (Psalm 19:1)

Notes:

1. Interview of Christopher Hitchens by Anderson Cooper, *Anderson Cooper 360*, CNN, May 15, 2007 http://transcripts.cnn.com/TRANSCRIPTS/0705/15/acd.01.html accessed 4-19-11.

2. Richard Dawkins, *The God Delusion* (Boston: Houghton Mifflin, 2006), 31.

3. Gayle Trotter, "Intimidating Intelligence Dims the Brights," *Evangel Magazine*, 28 March 2010 http://firstthings.com/blogs/evangel/2010/03/intimidating-intelligence, accessed 4-19-11.

4. "The Brights" - NPR Commentary by Steven Waldman September 4, 2003, http://www.the-brights.net/vision/essays/waldman_futrell_geisert_npr.html, accessed 4-19-11.

5. Ibid.

6. Antony Flew with Roy Abraham Varghese, *There Is a God—How the World's Most Notorious Atheist Changed His Mind* (New York, NY: Harper Collins, 2007).

7. http://www.freerepublic.com/focus/f-news/1298098/posts, accessed 4-21-11.

8. http://www.newstatesman.com/religion/2009/04/returning-to-religion, accessed 4-19-11.

9. Janie B. Cheaney, "Lost and found: Doctrine brings a famous atheist back to faith" (*World*, 06 June, 2009) http://www.worldmag.com/articles/15410, accessed 4-19-11.

10. Ibid.

11. Matthew Parris, "As an atheist, I truly believe Africa needs God: Missionaries, not aid money, are the solution to Africa's biggest problem—the crushing passivity of the people's mindset," *The Sunday Times* (December 27, 2008).

12. Peter Hitchens, *The Rage Against God: How Atheism Led Me to Faith* (Grand Rapids, MI: Zondervan Publishing, 2010).

13. Steven Pinker, *How the Mind Works*, (New York: W. W. Norton, 1997), 555.

14. Dinesh D'Souza, *What's So Great About Christianity?* (Washington, DC: Regnery Press, 2007).

15. Christopher Hitchens and Douglas Wilson, "Is Christianity Good For the World?" (*Christianity Today*, 03 Feb, 2011) http://www.christianitytoday.com/ct/2007/mayweb-only/119-12.0.html?start=4, accessed 4-19-11.

16. Flew, 76-77.

17. Richard Dawkins, *The God Delusion* (Boston: Houghton Mifflin, 2006), p. 273, 279.

18. Ibid., D'Souza, 214

19. Ibid., D'Souza, 221.

20. George Weigel, "Christian Number-Crunching," *First Things*, February 9, 2011. http://www.firstthings.com/onthesquare/2011/02/christian-number-crunching, accessed 4-20-11.

21. Alister McGrath, "The Twilight of Atheism," *Christianity Today* (February 28, 2005). http://www.christianitytoday.com/ct/2005/march/21.36.html, accessed 4-20-11.

22. Bertrand Russell, *The Autobiography of Bertrand Russell* (London: George Allen and Unwin, 1967), 146, cited by Roy Abraham Varghese in the Preface to Flew, *There Is a God*, xxi.

1. Read Psalm 19:1-6.

   a. What do the heavens "say"? (verse 1a)

   b. How are the "words" of heaven heard? What evidence is there that what they say is true? (verse 1a)

   c. What does the firmament reveal? (verse 1b)

   d. What can you see in the heavens that reveals the handiwork of God? (verse 1b)

   e. What does verse 2 say about the availability of this knowledge?

f. How does verse 3 answer the person who says, "We never heard this voice. We never received this knowledge."

g. What do the movements of the sun and other heavenly bodies say about how they are sustained? What keeps them on schedule? (verses 4c-6)

h. What is the answer of Scripture to the question of order in the universe? (Genesis 1:14-19)

i. What other purpose does the stability of the universe serve to demonstrate? (Jeremiah 31:35-37)

j. In light of this evidence, what justification does the atheist have for his beliefs?

k. How could you use these verses to encourage a person who doubts the existence of God?

2. Read Romans 1:18-20.

   a. What does the word "suppress" suggest about the continual energy it takes to deny the existence of God?

   b. In light of Psalm 19:2, how consistent and continual must the activity of suppression be carried out?

   c. Which is easier: to receive something that is plainly at hand or to deny it exists? Why do atheists persist in the harder task?

   d. What has God made plainly evident about Himself since the beginning of creation? (verse 20)

e. What excuse will atheists be able to offer about the evidence for the existence of God? (verse 20)

f. Why will all who deny the existence of God be without excuse in the day of judgment? (verse 19)

3. What does John 7:17 contribute to the discussion of knowing the truth of God? What is man's responsibility in knowing?

DID YOU KNOW?

Two key words in the lexicon of religion have their roots in the Greek of the New Testament. The English word "atheist" comes from the Greek word *atheos*, a combination of the negative prefix "*a*" and "*theos*" the word for God. It only appears once in the New Testament (Ephesians 2:12) where it is translated "without God." Literally, the negative prefix makes "God" mean "no God" or "without God." The English "agnostic" comes from the Greek word *agnostos*. Again, the negative prefix "*a*" combines with "*gnosis*" the word for knowledge. Therefore, agnostos means "without knowledge" or "unknown" (Acts 17:23). Today, an atheist believes there is no God while an agnostic believes it can't be known whether or not God exists.

...WHEN CHRISTIANS WOULDN'T KNOW THEY WERE IN A WAR

Selected Scriptures

In this lesson we will learn about Satan's character and his strategies in attacking Christians.

OUTLINE

Approaching the end of the age before Christ's return, we can expect an intensification of spiritual warfare. But too many Christians have failed to prepare themselves. In order to protect ourselves against the attacks of Satan, it is important to know who Satan is and what he does.

I. **Who Satan Is**
   A. Satan Is the Great Deceiver
   B. Satan Is the Great Divider
   C. Satan Is the Great Destroyer

II. **What Satan Does**
   A. The Strategy of Indifference
   B. The Strategy of Ignorance
   C. The Strategy of Infiltration
   D. The Strategy of Intervention
   E. The Strategy of Intimidation

From the beginning of time, war has been easy to define and identify—opposing armies had names, home territories, consistency in dress and weapons. Army A and Army B met on a battlefield, were engaged in skirmishes or battles, and moved from place to place geographically.

In the modern era, the Vietnam War introduced "guerilla warfare" and American forces weren't quite prepared for the change. Hit and run tactics, booby traps, soldiers dressed like civilians—it was a new kind of war. And today, in the modern war on terrorism, things have changed even more. Today, more than fighting against armies and soldiers, we are fighting against a religiously-inspired ideology where the chief weapons are fear and intimidation. This is a war in which there are no rules. Terrorists, we have learned, can appear to be normal citizens at one moment and soldiers the next.

Christians should understand the war on terrorism better than anyone since spiritual warfare shares many similarities. Satan and his demons are invisible, they play by their own rules, they set traps and ambushes, they use deceit and trickery, and their weapons are spiritual instead of physical. Sadly, even though every Christian is a target of Satan and his demons, not every Christian knows it. Too many Christians are ill-equipped to be victorious in the battle to which they have been called.

And the battle is on! First Timothy 4:1 says that in "latter times" many will give "heed to deceiving spirits and doctrines of demons." And Revelation 9:8-11 paints a frightening picture of how earth will suffer during the Tribulation when demons are given free rein to attack. I have read several recent news accounts of the Roman Catholic Church, both in Italy and in the United States, increasing its training for priests and bishops in the area of spiritual warfare and exorcism. Spiritual attacks are increasing throughout Christendom, in Catholic and Protestant settings alike.

Two thousand, six hundred years ago a small book was written that is still being read by military strategists today: *The Art of War* by Sun Tzu. Consider his words from chapter three:

- If you know the enemy and you know yourself, you need not fear the result of a hundred battles.

- If you know yourself but not the enemy, for every victory gained, you will suffer a defeat.

- If you know neither the enemy nor yourself, you will succumb in every battle.[1]

The key principle is the first: In battle, you must know yourself and your enemy! In spiritual warfare, the Christian's enemy is Satan and his demonic hordes: "For we do not wrestle against flesh and blood, but against principalities, against powers, against the rulers of the darkness of this age, against spiritual hosts of wickedness in the heavenly places" (Ephesians 6:12). Without knowing our enemy well enough to know his strategies, we are doomed to defeat.

One of the most important things to realize in spiritual warfare is that people are not our enemy. Satan is the enemy! Yes, Satan may use people in destructive or hurtful ways in our life. But if that happens and we attack the person, we are not attacking the enemy. Only defending ourselves against the true enemy will bring victory in spiritual warfare.

I once made a list from the Bible of all the verbs—the action words —associated with Satan. And it is a frightening list: He beguiles, seduces, opposes, resists, deceives, sows, hinders, buffets, tempts, persecutes, blasphemes, and does many more similar things. All his actions are deceitful, divisive, destructive, and they try to diminish and deface the glory of God. For the remainder of ths lesson, we will define who Satan is and what he does in an attempt to know the enemy.

WHO SATAN IS

Satan is three things: a deceiver, a divider, and a destroyer. Almost everything he does can be placed under one of these three headings.

Satan Is the Great Deceiver

John 8:44 is the classic text on this point: ". . . there is no truth in [Satan]. When he speaks a lie, he speaks from his own resources, for he is a liar and the father of it." We often say a person today speaks in his "native tongue" or "native language"—meaning the language they know best, the language in which they can conduct personal and commercial business. For Satan, that is the language of lies! There is no truth in him. Everything that comes from his mouth is intended to deceive since lies are his native tongue. The apostle John confirms this in Revelation 12:9: ". . . Satan, who deceives the whole world."

Satan Is the Great Divider

Satan's strategy is to divide and conquer. When he was cast out of heaven he took a third of the angels with him. He divided the first human family, pitting Cain against Abel. He tempted Ananias and Sapphira to divide their loyalty between God and money. Wherever you see Satan at work, you'll find division. Conversely, whenever you find disputes and division, you'll find Satan. And yes, Satan goes to church. In the first century, there was one Church; today there are hundreds of denominations resulting from divisions through the centuries. And the Church is weaker as a result. Satan delights in weakening and destroying by division.

So much division in the Church and elsewhere begins with words. James says the tongue "is set on fire by hell. . . . It is an unruly evil, full of deadly poison" (James 3:6, 8). When we find words hurting and dividing, guess who is delighted in those situations?

Satan Is the Great Destroyer

Satan will do anything to destroy, delay, demolish, or dismantle God's work. Job, from the Old Testament, is a prime example. When Satan was given access to Job he destroyed everything (including Job's health) except Job and his wife—he even destroyed Job's wife's attitude toward her husband. He will destroy everything he possibly can for the purpose of destroying the faith of the people of God. Satan knows he can't destroy God so his next tactic is to destroy the faith of the people of God. Fortunately, Job resisted and kept the faith and saw God bless him richly at the end of his test. In Revelation 9:11 Satan's "name in Hebrew is Abaddon, but in Greek he has the name Apollyon"—and both names in their respective languages mean destruction, or destroyer.

Warning: Satan will take any opportunity, however small and seemingly insignificant, to destroy a lifetime of faithfulness to God. Be on your guard.

WHAT SATAN DOES

In order to be on our guard we must know *how* Satan does his deceiving, dividing, and destroying work. This is war; we must believe our enemy has strategies he works against us.

The Strategy of Indifference

Satan wants nothing more than for you to be indifferent toward him, to think he doesn't exist. He will therefore do whatever he can to create that appearance. If he can make you think he's a cartoon figure created by Hollywood, with a red suit, pitchfork, horns, and pointed tail, he will. And it seems to be working.

A 2009 survey by the Barna Group asked 1,871 professing Christians whether or not they agreed that "Satan is not a living being, but a symbol of evil." Forty percent agreed, along with 19 percent more who agreed "somewhat," and eight percent who weren't sure what they believed. That means 67 percent of the professing Christians did not believe Satan is an actual spiritual being. Only 26 percent disagreed with nine percent disagreeing "somewhat."[2]

There are two reasons why it is easy for Satan to hide himself: First, he's invisible; second, he does his work through worldly means such as media, arts, politics, economics, and education. He even transforms himself into an "angel of light" (2 Corinthians 11:14), meaning he can do things that appear good. But the truth is that "the whole world lies under the sway of the wicked one" (1 John 5:19).

Why would the apostle Paul give us complete instructions on how to put on the armor of God if we were not at war with an actual, powerful spiritual being (Ephesians 6:10-18)? The word "against" appears six times in that passage. Who are we to "stand against" if not an actual being? Spiritual warfare is like standing in a rushing stream that is constantly, every second of every day of every year of your life, rushing against you. It never lets up.

In his book *This World: Playground or Battleground?*, A. W. Tozer described how serious Christians used to see this world as a battleground. Today, however, the spiritual world has become not a battleground, but a playground. Instead of being here to fight, we're here to frolic. Instead of being here to view earth as a foreign land, we've made ourselves very much at home here. Rather than living in expectation of eternity with God, we're pursuing life as we want it now with little thought for the future.[3]

Satan is delighted that we are taking him far less seriously than we used to.

The Strategy of Ignorance

In 1982 an American missionary and professor, Paul Hiebert, published a groundbreaking article titled "The Flaw of the Excluded Middle."[4] As a missionary to India he had discovered that he was ill-equipped to handle the spiritual realities that Indians took for granted—that realm between heaven and earth where spirits and humans encounter one another. He had been trained in the scientific method in America which didn't take into account that which could not be seen nor measured. The non-scientific Indian natives were the opposite: They knew full well that unseen powers exist. Hiebert's article was a call for Western missionary training to incorporate this unseen "excluded middle" into their worldview.

The problem in the West was ignorance. In the early 1980s, many theologically astute, evangelical missionary leaders (and other Christian leaders) knew little of what the Bible is clear about: There is a spiritual war taking place. It was as if leaders thought a giant glass canopy had been installed around planet Earth at the end of the first century preventing Satan and demons from having access to Christians. But in other cultures where science had not explained away supernatural phenomena, the war was all too real.

There is still too much ignorance in the Church today. There are still too many Christians who are suffering from spiritual attacks and have no idea why. God said, "My people are destroyed for lack of knowledge" (Hosea 4:6) for a reason.

The Strategy of Infiltration

If we are indifferent and ignorant about Satan, it is easy for him to infiltrate our lives. Resisting infiltration is pictured perfectly in Ephesians 4:26-27: "'Be angry, and do not sin': do not let the sun go down on your wrath, nor give place to the devil." Paul's point is obvious: Being angry unto sin is a good way to allow the devil to get a "foothold" *(NIV)* in your life. Sin of any kind is the devil's turf. If we willingly embrace sin and do not repent and keep a clean heart before God, it's like issuing an invitation to the devil—like giving him a "place" in our life. The principle is the same as in Proverbs 6:27: "Can a man take fire to his bosom, and his clothes not be burned?" If we play with fire we're going to get burned; if we play with sin we're going to get attacked by the devil.

The idea of a "place" or "foothold" comes from the rocky, mountainous terrain of the Bible lands. In order to gain entrance into an enemy stronghold built into the side of a mountain, warriors would have to climb—and a tiny toehold or foothold, big enough to insert a sandal, might make all the difference in capturing the stronghold. Satan will take any tiny advantage we give him—just enough to get his foot in the door of our life.

The Strategy of Intervention

The idea of staging an intervention in a person's life to arrest the progress of some kind of injurious or unwise behavior is well known. The goal is to intervene—to break the normal cycle of behavior and substitute clinical help or other better behaviors.

Just so, Satan loves to intervene in our lives to do just the opposite: distract us from our healthy spiritual behaviors and tempt us with bad behaviors. If he can distract us from the spiritually productive priorities in our life and occupy us with the things of this world, his intervention will be successful. If we are too busy to pray, study the Bible, serve others, attend church or Bible studies, then we will not grow spiritually. We will remain babes in Christ.

A devotional reading sent to me by a friend concludes with this question: "Have you figured out the difference between being busy and being successful in what God has called you to do? Sometimes being busy—B-U-S-Y—just means Being Under Satan's Yoke."[5] There's nothing wrong with being busy, of course, as long as we are busy with the right things. And as long as we don't get so busy that we begin to think of our busyness as a way of impressing God. Even that is a trap of Satan to distract us from true spirituality.

The Strategy of Intimidation

Some Christians are confused about the power of Satan and are intimidated by him; they believe Satan is the opposite counterpart of God.[6] That is false! Satan is in no way equal to God. As a created angel, Satan's opposite in heavenly places is Michael the archangel, not God.

Yes, Satan has powers we do not have, powers that must be respected. But they need not be feared. Why? Because "He who is in you is greater than he who is in the world" (1 John 4:4). The Holy Spirit who lives in us to manifest the life of the Lord Jesus Christ (Galatians 2:20) is far more powerful than Satan. Again referring to Ephesians 6 and the believer's spiritual armor—Paul would not have given us this armor and told us to use it if it were not sufficient to prevent our being destroyed by Satan. So there is no need to be intimidated by Satan—as long as we have our armor on and are filled with the Spirit.

Napoleon Bonaparte is said to have felt he could conquer the world if it were not for Britain, the nation that defeated him at

Waterloo. Satan is the same way. If he could rid history of the cross and resurrection of Jesus Christ, he too might conquer the world. First John 3:8 says, "For this purpose the Son of God was manifested, that He might destroy the works of the devil." Satan can't get rid of Jesus, but Jesus can destroy the works of the devil.

Notes:

1. Sun Tzu, *The Art of War* (Hollywood, FL: Simon & Brown, 2010), 11.

2. The Barna Group, "Most American Christians Do Not Believe that Satan or the Holy Spirit Exist," Barna.org, 10 April 2009, accessed 24 January 2010.

3. A. W. Tozer, *This World: Playground or Battleground?* (Camp Hill, PA: Christian Publications, Inc., 1989), Chapter 1.

4. Paul G. Hiebert, "The Flaw of the Excluded Middle." *Missiology* 10:35-47, January 1982. Reprinted in Ralph D. Winter and Steven C. Hawthorne (eds.), Perspectives on the World Christian Movement: *A Reader* (3rd edition) (Pasadena, CA: William Carey Library, 1999), 414-421.

5. Bob Gass, *The Word for Today,* September/October/November 2010 (Alphareta, GA: Bob Gass Ministries), 21.

6. Randy Alcorn, *If God is Good: Faith in the Midst of Suffering and Evil,* (Colorado Springs: Multnomah, 2009), 51.

1. Read 1 John 5:18-19.

   a. What does verse 19b say about Satan's domain, his area of influence?

   b. What evidence of his influence do you see in the world that would support verse 19b?

   c. Explain how verse 19b and Deuteronomy 10:14 can both be true?

   d. How far does Satan's influence in the world extend? (Use Job 1:12 and 2:6 as examples.)

   e. What security does verse 18 provide against the attacks of the devil?

f. Based on the promise of protection to "whoever is born of God," what does this suggest about the vulnerability of those not born again of God?

g. How do you know that the promise of verse 18 applies to you?

2. What do you think it means to be a "son of the devil" as described in John 8:44 and Acts 13:10?

a. In what ways would the normal resemblance between fathers and sons apply in this spiritual realm?

b. What insight does this spiritual father-son metaphor offer to the New Testament idea of "adoption"? (Romans 8:15; Ephesians 1:5)

c. By whom have Christians been adopted?

3. What two words precede the phrase "of the devil" in Ephesians 6:11 and 2 Timothy 2:26?

   a. What do these two words suggest about the character and strategies of Satan?

   b. What do they suggest about the need to practice the admonition of 1 Peter 5:8?

4. Read Ephesians 6:10-18.

   a. What does verse 10 suggest as to the purpose of what follows? What is the purpose of spiritual armor? (verse 10)

b. How is that purpose expressed in more detail in verse 11b?

c. How does verse 12 dispel the notion that we are at war with the "idea" of evil?

d. List the six elements of armor in verses 14-17 and what each represents as a spiritual weapon.

e. What do the first two words of verse 11 and the first word of verse 14 suggest about the believer's role in his own defense?

DID YOU KNOW?

Christians often wonder if they can be demon-possessed? The answer is no. Unlike non-believers (Matthew 4:24; 8:16, 28), there are no examples in the New Testament of Christians being described as possessed by a demon. In fact, the Greek word used in these instances is not literally translated as "demon-possessed." *Daimonizomai* is best translated as "demonized," or demon-influenced or afflicted. If a person has no spiritual or moral defense mechanisms to use in resisting the devil, then yes—that person could be completely dominated by Satan's influence, or "possessed." Christians can be influenced (tempted, harassed) by Satan and his demons but not dominated due to the presence of the Holy Spirit.

...WHEN JESUS WOULD BE SO PROFANED

Hebrews 1:1-3

In this lesson we discover why Jesus deserves praise instead of profanity in our culture.

OUTLINE

Not long ago in America, Jesus Christ was honored and respected as the One worshipped by the majority of citizens. But today Jesus and His name are profaned throughout our culture, especially in entertainment. Once Jesus is known for who He is, profanity will turn to praise.

I. **Jesus: The Final Word From God**

II. **Jesus: The First Cause of Creation**

III. **Jesus: The Fullness of the Godhead**

IV. **Jesus: The Facilitator of All Things**

V. **Jesus: The Forgiveness of Our Sins**

VI. **Jesus: The Finisher of Our Faith**

VII. **Jesus: Our Faithful High Priest**

If you are a consumer of contemporary media, you have seen Jesus Christ appear more and more frequently—and not usually in an edifying way. For example, on January 13, 2011, Stephen Colbert, the host of the Comedy Central show *The Colbert Report*, included Jesus in a comedy sketch. He was spoofing a Doritos corn chip ad that was part of a contest to choose a Doritos ad that would appear during the 2011 Super Bowl. This ad didn't win and so was not broadcast nationally, but it was part of Colbert's show that night and was rebroadcast all across the Internet.

In the ad, a priest decides to replace the communion bread with Doritos to boost attendance at his service. In his spoof, Colbert didn't see why Doritos couldn't be a substitute for communion wafers since they are both unleavened. He referenced Mark 14:20 which refers to one of the disciples "dipping" with Jesus in the bowl at the last supper: "Therefore, Jesus was a chip!" He went on to say how Jesus "snackrified" Himself for our sins, eliciting gales of laughter from the audience.[1] But I noticed no public outcry from Christians over the inclusion of their Savior in this demeaning comedy sketch.

Including Jesus in profane media situations is so common in America that hardly anyone pays attention or gets upset—including Christians. His image appears on clothing and He is made into a cartoon character on profane television shows like *The Simpsons* and *South Park*. In a 2010 interview, pop star Elton John said, "I think Jesus was a compassionate, super-intelligent gay man who understood human problems."[2] There is, of course, absolutely no historical basis for such a statement, but people today have no problem with making untrue statements about Christ that are sure to be offensive.

The list of ways Jesus has been incorporated for ideological and profit-motivated reasons goes on and on. In their book, *Dethroning Jesus: Exposing Popular Culture's Quest to Unseat the Biblical Christ*, scholars Darrell Bock and Daniel Wallace explained that the popular view of Jesus today is not biblical Christianity, it's "Jesusanity":

> "Jesusanity is a coined term for the alternative story about Jesus Christ. Here the center of the story is still Jesus, but Jesus as a prophet or a teacher of religious wisdom. His role is primarily one of teacher, and guide, and example. Jesus' special status involves His insight into the human condition and the enlightenment He brings to it. In this story, the key is that Jesus inspires others, but there's no throne for Jesus. He is One

among many—the best perhaps—and certainly One we can learn from and follow."[3]

I never thought I'd see the day in America when Jesus Christ was fair game for comedians and commercial entrepreneurs, especially those who profess to believe in Him like the self-confessed, devout Roman Catholic Stephen Colbert. I'm not picking on Mr. Colbert. Indeed, I have seen far worse examples of the profaning of Jesus Christ. But he is a good example of how easy it is, even for Christ-followers, to get squeezed into the mold of the world if we are not careful.

The Jesus we need to know will not be found in modern media. Pastor John Piper has said,

"To the degree that the church is trained to distrust the Jesus of the Gospels and to look for ever new human creations of Christ, the real Jesus is blurred, and his power to break free from the unbiblical traditions that bind him is blunted."[4]

Cultural messages are like elevator music—we're listening without really listening; we sometimes don't even realize the music is playing until we find ourselves in the elevator alone and we suddenly notice it. And later that day we find ourselves humming the song we heard. We didn't ask for it or seek it out, but now it's there. And false media messages about Jesus Christ get into our subconscious the same way and, over time, dull our sensitivity. We may even find ourselves laughing along with the crowd without realizing the implications of our actions.

In this lesson we are going to look at the biblical image of Jesus Christ. The first place to learn about Jesus in the New Testament is the four Gospel accounts of Matthew, Mark, Luke, and John. But the next best place is the book of Hebrews—there is more about Jesus in Hebrews than in any other New Testament book outside the Gospels.

Hebrews was written to first-century Jewish Christians who were under extreme pressure because of their faith. Indeed, they were on the verge of giving up, of recanting their faith in Christ. So the writer of Hebrews appeals to the believers to keep their faith anchored firmly in the reality of who Jesus Christ is. Only a complete and accurate picture of who Jesus is will be enough to turn back the pressure of persecution. That first-century message is one we need for the twenty-first century as well— we know not what pressures are ahead for us.

The main point of Hebrews is clearly identified for us: "Now this is the main point of the things we are saying: We have such a

High Priest, who is seated at the right hand of the throne of the Majesty in the heavens (Hebrews 8:1)." The book is all about Jesus; how He is better than everything and everyone that had come before. "Better" occurs 13 times in Hebrews to demonstrate that Jesus is the zenith of God's revelation to man: better than the angels, Moses, Joshua, the Old Covenant—better than everything. The use of "better" in Hebrews is reminiscent of the proverbial marketing slogan, "The best just got better." It's not that what came before was bad; it's that what we have now is superior or better.

JESUS: THE FINAL WORD FROM GOD (HEBREWS 1:1-2A)

Before God spoke *finally* in Christ, He spoke in "various times and in various ways . . . in time past to the fathers through the prophets." Beginning with Adam, God spoke all the way through the Old Testament—a little here, a little there. Each revelation was important and each was complete for the purpose for which it was given. But God never spoke everything to or through one person or prophet. If you put all the fragments together, you have the Old Testament. But there was still more to be said.

God "has in these last days spoken to us by His Son." It is no surprise that one of the words used to describe Jesus is "the Word" —the Word that "was God" (John 1:1). Jesus is God's last Word to man in terms of understanding. Yes, the books of the Old Testament were inspired and written prior to Jesus' ministry on earth, chronologically speaking. But when we say "last" we're talking about the finality of revelation. Jesus was the One the prophets wrote about and looked for. There is nothing else that needs to be revealed in terms of God's plan for mankind. We don't need to look anywhere else for further revelation about God's plan of salvation. Jesus is God's final Word.

JESUS: THE FIRST CAUSE OF CREATION (HEBREWS 1:2C)

We are then told that Jesus is the One through whom God created all things. In Genesis 1 we read, "In the beginning God created the heavens and the earth." But in Hebrews we learn that the member of the Trinity directly responsible was Christ: "through whom [Christ] also He [God] made the worlds" (verse 2c). The apostle John tells us the same thing: "All things were made through Him, and without Him nothing was made that was made" (John 1:3). And the apostle Paul confirms: "For by Him [Christ] all things were created that are in heaven and that are on earth" (Colossians 1:16a). And Paul adds an interesting note: "All things were created through Him and for Him" (Colossians 1:16b). You and I were created for Jesus Christ, along with everything else in this world. It all belongs to Him.

JESUS: THE FULLNESS OF THE GODHEAD (HEBREWS 1:3A)

The writer to the Hebrews then tells us that Jesus is "the brightness of [God's] glory and the express image of His person." This is the same as what the apostle Paul says in Colossians 1:19: "For it pleased the Father that in [Christ] all the fullness [of God] should dwell." And Paul wrote to Timothy that "God was manifested in the flesh" in Christ (1 Timothy 3:16). Jesus Himself said, "He who has seen Me has seen the Father" (John 14:9). One of the most amazing statements is what God the Father says about the Son: "But to the Son He says: 'Your throne, O God, is forever and ever'" (Hebrews 1:8). God the Father calls God the Son "God"! These are clear statements about the deity of Christ. He is not just a good man, He is the God-Man!

Many people who admire the brilliance of the founding father, Thomas Jefferson (and rightly so), are not aware of his attitude toward Jesus Christ. Jefferson produced what is now called *The Jefferson Bible*, a version of the life and teachings of Christ that removed any references to His deity, miracles, the Trinity, angels, the Resurrection—almost everything except Jesus' teaching on morality and ethics. Marilyn Mellowes, writing for the PBS show *Frontline*, said, "In short, Mr. Jefferson's Jesus, modeled on the ideals of the Enlightenment thinkers of his day, bore a striking resemblance to Jefferson himself."[5]

But that doesn't change who Jesus is. He is who the Bible says He is in the verses you just read, not who we want Him to be.

JESUS: THE FACILITATOR OF ALL THINGS (HEBREWS 1:3B)

If you've ever wondered who keeps our chaotic world from flying apart, from coming completely unglued, it is Jesus. He is the one who is "upholding all things by the word of His power." Scientists will tell us in their scientific language why our planet stays on track day after day, but the Bible's answer is much simpler: Jesus. Here's how the apostle Paul put it in Colossians 1:17: "And He is before all things, and in Him all things consist."

Since the beginning of the creation He put in motion, that creation has held together—"consisted"—in Christ. It was His power that caused it to exist, and it is by His power it consists.

JESUS: THE FORGIVENESS OF OUR SINS (HEBREWS 1:3C)

The most important facet of Christ's jewel-like person is that He is the One who forgives our sins: "when He had by Himself purged our sins." Christ is not only the revealer of God, He is the Redeemer of men.

Hebrews is filled with language of the Old Testament that the Jewish-Christian readers would immediately understand. Around 10 times in the Old Testament, the word "purge" is used to picture the cleansing of sin, the removal of unrighteousness. And that is what ultimately makes Jesus better than the Old Testament sacrifices. "By Himself" He took away our sins forever—something the Old Testament priests with the blood of tens of thousands of animals could not do. That was the chief reason for Jesus' coming to earth: "to give His life as a ransom for many" (Mark 10:45).

Hebrews 9 goes into great detail on the way sins were cleansed under the Old Covenant—how the priests would enter the Holy Place year after year with the blood of bulls and goats to make atonement for the people's sins. "But now, once at the end of the ages, He has appeared to put away sin by the sacrifice of Himself" (Hebrews 9:26b). Everything else that Jesus is—the Creator, the fullness of God, the One who holds things together—all of that leads to the purpose of His coming to earth: to take away our sins once and for all.

JESUS: THE FINISHER OF OUR FAITH (HEBREWS 1:3)

Christ is the finisher of our faith. After removing our sins once and for all, Christ "sat down at the right hand of the Majesty on high." That's another Old Testament reference: In the tabernacle, and later the temple in Jerusalem, the high priest was never allowed to sit down. Among all the furniture in the temple, there was no chair because the work of atonement was never finished; it was repeated year after year. But Christ sat down in heaven at the right hand of the Father because atonement for sin was finished! There is nothing you or I can do to the salvation process to add to what Christ has done. "It is finished!" (John 19:30)

Jesus: Our Faithful High Priest (Hebrews 2:17-18)

It is amazing to consider that One with the divine résumé of Christ could also act on such a personal level as to be our high priest—but He does. But to be our high priest, "He had to be made like His brethren . . . to make propitiation for the sins of the people" (Hebrews 2:17). The high priest in the Old Testament was a human representative of sinful people who offered up "sinless" sacrifices (animals without blemish). Christ became like us but offered up Himself as a sinless sacrifice for our sins. He became a personal high priest and sacrifice at the same time.

In becoming "like His brethren" Jesus was "being tempted . . . to aid those who are tempted" (verse 18). Hebrews 4:15 says, "For we do not have a High Priest who cannot sympathize with our weaknesses, but was in all points tempted as we are, yet without sin." Jesus experienced real temptation but resisted the temptation in order that He might qualify to be our High Priest—and to intercede for us at the right hand of the Father (Hebrews 7:25; 1 John 2:1). Because Jesus never yielded to the temptation to sin, He qualified to be a sacrifice pleasing to God (the "lamb of God"; John 1:29). And because He knows what it is like to undergo temptation, He can intercede for us and be our advocate before the Father.

I hope you have concluded by now that I recommend Jesus to you! He may be reviled and profaned in our culture, but He stands above all others in who He is and what He came to accomplish. Through faith in Him, you can know that He serves as your perfect and personal High Priest—the best God has ever done for those He created.

Notes:

1. http://www.colbertnation.com/the-colbert-report-videos/371019/january-13-2011/thought-for-food—fruit-pouch—doritos-ad—super-big-gulp, accessed 2-11-11.

2. Sonia Gallego, "Elton John: Jesus 'Super-Intelligent Gay Man'." February 19, 2010, abcnews.com. http://abcnews.go.com/Entertainment/elton-john-jesus-super-intelligent-gay-man/story?id=9889098, accessed 5-28-2011.

3. Darrel Bock and Daniel Wallace, *Dethroning Jesus: Exposing Popular Culture's Quest to Unseat the Biblical Christ*, (Nashville: Thomas Nelson, Inc., 2007), 4.

4. John Piper, *What Jesus Demands from the World* (Wheaton, IL: Crossway Books, 2006), p. 35.

5. tp://www.pbs.org/wgbh/pages/frontline/shows/religion/jesus/jefferson.html, accessed 2-17-11.

1. Read Colossians 1:13-20.

   a. Verses 15-20 are about Christ's supremacy. What great event is described in verses 13-14 that require Christ's supremacy to be explained?

   b. What do we have in Christ that could not be found in any other? (verse 14)

   c. Of whom is Christ the image? (verse 15a)

   d. Compare verse 15a with Genesis 1:26-27. Who was first designated as "the image of God"?

   e. How is Christ qualified to be called "the image of God"? What makes Him different from Adam and Eve in Genesis 3?

   f. In whose image is Adam and Eve's son, Seth, said to have been born? (Genesis 5:3)

   g. What changed from Genesis 1 to Genesis 5 that required the change in the "image" language (from image of God to image of man)?

h. How is Christ compared to the first Adam in 1 Corinthians 15:22, 45?

i. Why is it appropriate for the sinless Christ to be called "the last Adam"? (1 Corinthians 15:45)

j. How do the words "last" (1 Corinthians 15:45), "sat down" (Hebrews 1:3), and "finished" (John 19:30) convey the same message?

k. How does Romans 8:29 help explain the idea of Christ as the "firstborn over all creation"? (verse 15b)

l. How does "created . . . for Him" contribute to the notion of creation stewardship found in Genesis 1:28? Whose property is creation?

m. Compare "consist" in verse 17 with Paul's words in Acts 17:28. What are the implications for you personally of knowing that Christ is that omnipresent?

n. How does "firstborn from the dead" give you hope about life after death? What if it said "only-born" instead of "firstborn"?

o. What significance do you find in Paul mentioning the "last Adam" and our resurrection in such close proximity? (1 Corinthians 15:45, 51-58) How are they connected?

2. What could you do to elevate the posture of Christ in our culture in terms of your response to events in the media and the comments of friends and co-workers?

DID YOU KNOW?

The Book of Hebrews is the only Bible book that has "God" as its first word in English translations. The original Greek text begins with two adverbs and literally reads: "Many times and many ways long ago God spoke to the fathers by the prophets." But in English all of verse one (except "God") is a dependent clause —the verb associated with God doesn't appear until verse 2: "God . . . has . . . spoken. . . ." The first word in most other New Testament letters is the name of the author: "Paul . . . to the church of God in Corinth" (1 Corinthians 1:1-2). This sets Hebrews apart as different again since the author's name is never mentioned. There is, therefore, no conclusive evidence as to the identity of the author.

...When Marriage Would Be Obsolete

Selected Scriptures

In this lesson we note the alarming changes to the institution of marriage in America.

OUTLINE

Just a few decades ago most of society agreed on the definition of marriage: one man and one woman joined together for a lifetime. Today marriage has become an option in our culture. But changing or ignoring God's ordinances has serious implications for societies that do so.

I. **Discerning the Meaning of Marriage**

II. **Depreciating the Magnitude of Marriage**

III. **Dispelling Some Myths About Marriage**

IV. **Discovering the Motivations for Marriage**

V. **Deconstructing God's Mandate for Marriage**

VI. **Defending a Meaningful Marriage**
   A. Marriage Is a Product of Creation
   B. Marriage Is a Partnership Between One Man and One Woman
   C. Marriage Is a Permanent Union
   D. Marriage Is Primarily a Spiritual Union
   E. Marriage's Priority Is Procreation
   F. Marriage Is the Principle Building Block of Society

When Prince William of England and Kate Middleton, his fiancée, decided to begin living together several months before they were married, they unknowingly provided an excuse for other young couples who want to do the same: "If it's okay for the future king and queen of England to live together before marriage, why can't we?"

It's a good question—especially in light of the Queen's position: She is the designated head of the Church of England. She is a regular church attender and probably knows full well what the Bible teaches about marriage, yet she appears to have given her approval—along with the next king, Prince Charles, William's father. If they can be faithful members of the Church of England and ignore what the Bible teaches about sex outside of marriage, why shouldn't everyone else?

I don't single out Prince William, Kate Middleton, or the royal family to pick on them. Rather they serve as an excellent example of how the biblical standards of marriage are being altered by modern societies—even the heads of entire Christian denominations like the Queen of England. Not only is maintaining a chaste relationship prior to marriage no longer "necessary," but the whole notion of marriage itself is now deemed optional. We can be thankful that Prince William and Ms. Middleton at least followed through in a public ceremony of marriage commitment.

A journalist at MSNBC.com wrote this about the "royal shack-up" (their terms): "If Her Majesty's loyal subjects are aghast at the disclosure that William and Kate had been cohabiting [for eight months], they haven't shown it. But then again, it's 2010."[1]

I never thought I'd see the day when marriage would be considered obsolete.

DISCERNING THE MEANING OF MARRIAGE

Queen Elizabeth described 1992 as a "horrible year" in her reign. It was no doubt due in part to the break-up of three of her children's marriages: two divorces and one separation that ended in divorce in 1993. Perhaps that's why Prince William and his fiancée received the royal blessing to live together before they married—in hopes of preventing another failed marriage.

Unfortunately, studies show that living together before marriage is not a guarantee of marital permanence. Historically, cohabitation has been an indicator of the likelihood of marriage failure, not marriage success. The future will reveal whether that trend continues, but one trend is certain: More and more couples are making marriage optional; more and more couples are living together, even having children, without getting married. In 1977, fewer than one million opposite sex couples were living together while unmarried. In 2007, there were 6.4 million couples cohabiting.[2]

There is no question that the definition of marriage has changed in American society, including why marriage is important. America's definition used to be consistent with the biblical definition, but that is no longer true.

DEPRECIATING THE MAGNITUDE OF MARRIAGE

One national survey found that 44 percent of Americans in the traditional marrying age range (18-29) responded "Yes" when asked if marriage was becoming obsolete.[3] The people who say that marriage is obsolete have no idea of the long-term implications of removing from society something God has ordained.

For instance, in 1973 the Supreme Court made lawful the taking of unborn human life from a mother's womb. While that seemed to be an easy legal decision at the time, it has resulted in more than 53 million human beings missing from the life of the nation. That is an incalculable loss! Today, nearly four decades later, our Social Security system is soon to be broke because (in part) 53 million wage earners have gone missing; people who would otherwise have paid into Social Security during their working years are not here. That's an example of how we reap what we sow (Galatians 6:7).[4]

Social engineering decisions are easier to make than their consequences are to live with. America has a dark spot of guilt on its national conscience because of the killing of 53 million (and counting) human babies. Regardless of whether individuals have found forgiveness from God for their participation in that sin, the nation has never repented. Therefore, know it or not, we are a nation guilty of murder. And no nation can live a free and productive life when it is guilty of unresolved and unforgiven sins.

Marriage will become a similar situation if America continues to make marriage optional. Marriage is a God-ordained institution that cannot be discarded without paying a price. God's Word has very specific things to say about making promises like those people make to one another in marriage. Basically, don't make promises if you don't intend to keep them (Ecclesiastes 5:2-6a; Matthew 5:37). Yet everyday in America thousands of people take back the vows they made in marriage. Just as with abortion, America *as a people* has a guilty conscience over matters that are acceptable in man's sight but not in God's. Yes, God forgives. But not everyone seeks His forgiveness; and as a nation, we certainly have not.

A writer for *Time* magazine wrote, "There is no other single force causing as much measurable hardship and financial misery in this country as the collapse of marriage."[5]

Back in December of 2010, the annual *State of Our Unions* report was released jointly by the National Marriage Project of the University of Virginia. The subtitle for the report reads, "When Marriage Disappears: The New Middle America." It says in part,

> "Marriage is not merely a private arrangement between two persons. It is a core social institution, an institution that helps to ensure the economic and social and emotional welfare of countless children and women and men in this nation . . . And so, the disappearance of marriage in Middle America would endanger the American Dream, the emotional and social welfare of children, and the stability of the social fabric in thousands of communities across the country."[6]

Those implications, like the implications of abortion, only become evident over time. But it is serious. In the words of the Pew report, "It's no small thing when nearly four-in-ten Americans agree that the world's most enduring social institution is becoming obsolete."[7] Historians may look back one day and conclude that the unraveling in America was a key contributor to her demise as a great nation.

DISPELLING SOME MYTHS ABOUT MARRIAGE

Dispelling some myths about marriage leads to a bit of good news. First, the divorce rate is not "50 percent" as is usually cited. Better research now says that the divorce rate in America has never exceeded 41 percent and will likely never reach 50 percent.[8]

Second, divorce rates among Christians have, in recent years, been said to mirror those of the general public. If we distinguish between truly committed Christian couples—those practicing biblical spiritual disciplines and living an active Christian life—and those who are just Christian in name only, there is a difference. Truly committed Christian couples "enjoy significantly lower divorce rates than mere church members." Committed Christian couples are 35 percent less likely to divorce than couples who are not serious followers of Christ.[9]

A third myth is that divorce is the biggest contemporary threat to marriage. In reality, cohabitation is a bigger threat. Between 1969 and 2009, the percentages of Americans who thought that living together before marriage ("shacking up," as it was called) was wrong has reversed itself: 68 percent thought it was wrong in 1969; 60 percent now believe it is not wrong.[10] Those numbers explain why so many people today are living together without being married.

DISCOVERING THE MOTIVATIONS FOR MARRIAGE

Marriage according to God is one man, one woman united spiritually, emotionally, physically, publicly, and legally, in a lifetime bond of loyal love for procreation, channeling sexual and emotional energy, and serving as a civilizing and stabilizing factor in society. But that definition is being radically challenged today. Very few people today consider marriage to be one man and one woman forever. Marriage and family have become subject to personal definitions. People are bonding for personal and emotional reasons rather than for the traditional reasons of having children, financial stability, division of labor, and others. Thus, when feelings change, people feel free to abandon whatever level of commitment they entered into. Research statistics aren't perfect, but they do provide a general picture of trends. And the trend today is *not* toward a biblical definition of marriage or motivation for getting married.

DECONSTRUCTING GOD'S MANDATE FOR MARRIAGE

In response to those in our society who are redefining and deconstructing the traditional marriage union, Dr. Albert Mohler has these thoughts:

> "We need to understand that marriage is not primarily about what we as individuals think we want or need. It is about a central public commitment that the society needs, that couples need, that children need, and yes, that the spouses need. Marriage is a public institution, not merely a private commitment. It identifies the couple as a pair committed to lifelong marriage and thus to be respected in this commitment. The fact that our

society has weakened marriage offers only further incentive to get it right and to strengthen this vital institution.

"The traditions of the wedding ceremony are important as a part of solemnizing and recognizing this covenanted relationship —but the traditions are expendable. Marriage is not. There is a universe of difference between a private promise and a public pledge. Marriage is about a public vow made by the man to the woman and the woman to the man whereby they become now husband and wife."[11]

Defending a Meaningful Marriage

There are six reasons for defending the traditional (biblical) view of marriage.

Marriage Is a Product of Creation

God didn't create a mass of human beings and then start pairing them off as a way to bring order out of chaos. Rather, He created a woman for the first man in order to complete him. Marriage is fundamental to human existence. A synergy results in the new "one flesh" (Genesis 2:24) that is greater than what either of the two individuals could produce living alone. Marriage is a prerequisite for populating the earth and is part of the creation order. To attempt to function in the creation without marriage as the basis is to invite dysfunction.

Marriage Is a Partnership Between One Man and One Woman

The definition of marriage in Genesis 2:24 could not be more clear: a partnership between a single man and a single woman. Not between multiples of either or between singles or multiples of the same sex. All of the confusion in contemporary cultures over the definition of marriage and a family stems from ignoring this basic creation principle. It doesn't matter how many people, or how many courts, or how many legislators attempt to redefine marriage by law or by practice, God's design cannot be changed. The society that changes something as fundamental as God's definition of marriage will reap the sad results as America is experiencing today.

Marriage Is a Permanent Union

When two become one, it was never intended that they become two again. Yes, divorces were granted in the Old Testament (Deuteronomy 24:1-4) but only because of "the hardness of [their] hearts" (Matthew 19:8), as Jesus told the Pharisees in His day. Jesus

Himself said, "Therefore what God has joined together, let not man separate" (Matthew 19:6). As is often said, "The exception proves the rule." For Moses and Jesus even to have provided an exception to the permanent union of marriage proves that the rule of permanence was the norm. Yet today, marriages are ended daily as individuals or couples decide that they have "fallen out of love."

Marriage Is Primarily a Spiritual Union

The rising trend in cohabitation today is due to couples having the three primary dimensions of marriage—spiritual, emotional, physical—backward. They feel they must live together physically to make sure they are sexually compatible. If that works, then they extend the relationship to determine emotional (personality) compatibility. Then, if ever, spirituality comes into view. That is exactly opposite to God's plan! Spiritual compatibility must always come first according to Scripture (2 Corinthians 6:14-18). If that dimension of compatibility is there, then the others will follow. As popular speaker Josh McDowell used to tell young people in his talks on sexuality, "The plumbing will always work! You don't need to try it out beforehand."

Marriage's Priority Is Procreation

Even with couples who choose to marry, one aspect is being forgotten: Procreation is marriage's priority. God's original commission to His human creatures was, "Be fruitful and multiply"—both in the Garden of Eden (Genesis 1:28) and after the Flood (Genesis 9:1). Yet today couples are having fewer children than in the past. The Pew surveys (mentioned earlier) found that 93 percent of Americans said that love was the primary reason for getting married—a first in recorded human history. Marrying for love alone creates huge problems—it opens the door for any individuals or groups to marry since they love one another. Love is important, of course, but not more so than procreation between a man and a woman.

Marriage Is the Principle Building Block of Society

Marriage is the only "organization" instituted by God in the Garden of Eden, making it the core building block for human society on earth. Marriages are the glue that holds successive generations together. They serve as a way to channel sexual and emotional energy which might otherwise be destructive in society. And fathers and mothers (and grandparents) provide wisdom and instruction for future generations.

Wherever you are in your life relative to marriage, I urge you to make marriage the priority in your life that God intended it to be —for God's glory, for the good of your children and future generations, and for the preservation of our society.

Notes:

1. "Royal Shack-Up: Kate and William moved in months ago." http://today.msnbc.msn.com/id/40253368/ns/today-today_people, accessed 3-2-11.

2. Sharon Jayson, "Census reports more unmarried couples living together," *USA Today*, July 28, 2008. http://www.usatoday.com/news/nation/census/2008-07-28-cohabitation-census_N.htm accessed 3-3-11.

3. Pew Social Trends Staff, "The Decline of Marriage and Rise of New Families, *Pew Research Center.com*, 18 November 2010, http://pewsocialtrends.org/2010/11/18/the-decline-of-marriage-and-rise-of-new-families/3/ accessed 9 December 2010.

4. For more details on the economic impact of abortion, see http://www.nrlc.org/Factsheets/FS04_MissingPersons.pdf, accessed 3-7-11.

5. Caitlin Flanagan, "Is There Hope for the American Marriage?" *Time.com.*, 2 July 2009, http://www.time.com/time/nation/article/0,8599,1908243,00.html, accessed 27 December 2010.

6. *The State of Our Unions, Marriage in America 2010: When Marriage Disappears: The New Middle America*, W. Bradford Wilcox, editor, December 2010, http://www.stateofourunions.org/2010/SOOU2010.pdf, accessed 11 January 2011, xi; 52.

7. Ibid, Pew.

8. Dan Hurley, "Divorce Rate: It's Not as High as You Think." *NYT.com*, April 19, 2005. http://www.nytimes.com/2005/04/19/health/19divo.html?_r'1, accessed 3-8-11.

9. Glenn T. Stanton. A First-Person: The Christian divorce rate myth (what you've heard is wrong) @ *Baptist Press*, February 15, 2011. http://www.bpnews.net/BPnews.asp?ID'34656 accessed 3-8-11.

10. Pew.

11. Albert Mohler, "Does Marriage Matter." *AlbertMohler.com*, Jan 15, 2008. http://www.albertmohler.com/2008/01/15/does-marriage-matter/, accessed 3-10-11.

1. Read Genesis 2:19-24.

   a. What happened in the Garden just before the creation of Eve that illustrated the necessity of a partner in life for Adam? (versus 19-20)

   b. How was Eve created? (verses 21-22)

   c. What did this unusual creative act symbolize in terms of the man and woman and their union as partners?

   d. On whom does God place the responsibility for leaving home and establishing a new family unit? (verse 24)

   e. In what different ways is it important for a man to leave his father and mother?

f. What does the order of words imply—can a man be "joined" to his wife if he has not first "left"? Why or why not?

g. Expand on the concept of "one flesh"—what meanings can this have in addition to physical oneness?

2. Read Matthew 19:1-12.

a. What was the intent of the Pharisees who came to Jesus? (verse 3)

b. In verse 9, how did Jesus narrow and specify the general instruction of Moses concerning divorce? (See Deuteronomy 24:1.)

c. What was the sole condition Jesus said could constitute grounds for divorce? (verse 9)

d. If a man divorced his wife for any other reason and remarried, what was he committing? (verse 9)

e. How do we know divorce is not God's best in any case? (verse 8)

f. Who, in your understanding, are those who "are able" to accept God's standards for marriage? (verse 12)

g. How do Jesus' words in Matthew 11:15 and 13:9 parallel this statement? Why was Jesus consistently calling out those who were ready to understand and apply kingdom values?

h. Apart from the doctrine of marriage, what support for the historicity of the Old Testament do you find in Jesus' words in verses 4-5?

On February 23, 2011, the Attorney General of the United States, at the direction of President Obama, announced that the administration would no longer defend the Defense of Marriage Act (DOMA) when it is challenged in U.S. courts. Long opposed by President Obama, DOMA is U.S. law, passed overwhelmingly by both houses of Congress and signed into law by President Clinton in 1996. The law says that no state has to recognize same-sex marriages that were made legal in any other state. DOMA also defined marriage as "a legal union between one man and one woman as husband and wife."

...WHEN MORALITY WOULD BE IN FREEFALL

Selected Scriptures

In this lesson we explore how our culture has lost its moral bearings and the true meaning of morality.

OUTLINE

Society is continually unveiling a "new normal" when it comes to morality. Things unacceptable generations ago are now tolerated and accepted. And the Church has become infected with the new morality. But God still has moral standards that He expects His people to keep.

I. **Shifting Moral Standards of Christians**

II. **The Solid Moral Foundation for Christians**
   A. Internalizing the Law
   B. Affirming the Law
   C. Sharpening the Law
   D. Honoring the Law

III. **Strength and Light by the Law**

IV. **The Spirit of God's Law**
   A. The Meaning of Murder
   B. The Meaning of Adultery
   C. The Meaning of Divorce
   D. The Meaning of Oaths
   E. The Meaning of Conflict
   F. The Meaning of Enemies

Early in 2011, a star player for the Brigham Young University basketball team was removed from the team, effectively ruining any hopes the team had of making it to the NCAA "Final Four" tournament. The player had violated the university's honor code which is signed by every student at the university.

There was immediate pushback from the sports media over removing a star player from the team, but the university stood its ground. And the media, in time, came around. An *ESPN* columnist wrote, "What makes this such a powerful testament is the fact that so many schools have cravenly abandoned their standards at such a time as this, embracing athletic expediency over institutional principle. It happens so often that we don't even raise an eyebrow at it anymore. Player arrests or other antisocial behaviors are minimized as youthful mistakes, with strenuous institutional effort put into counterspinning [*sic*] any negative publicity."[1]

Many schools have honor codes dealing with academics, but the BYU code is all-encompassing; it covers every aspect of a student's life on campus including spiritual matters since BYU is religiously-affiliated. Even non-Mormon students are expected to adhere to the code with the exception of mandatory church attendance.

A *Sports Illustrated*/CBS News 2010 investigation on crime in college football found that many top-ranked teams had players who had committed crimes.[2] But I don't recall hearing anything about those players being benched or removed from their teams. It seems that athletics is only one realm in which America has lost her moral compass.

I'm not picking on athletes here—just citing them as a highly visible symptom of a systemic problem in our culture: America has lost her moral way. If immorality is rampant in universities and colleges, then it is certainly rampant across the board in other strata of our culture. A recent *60 Minutes* episode highlighted the state of Pennsylvania's decision to legalize gambling to make up state budget shortfalls. Gambling is a losing venture in which the "house" (the state, in this case) always wins. The governor, Ed Rendell, defended the decision on the grounds that Pennsylvania's residents were going to "lose their paychecks" in casinos in neighboring states so they might as well lose them in Pennsylvania so the state could benefit. He claimed it is a "decent way to raise revenue."[3] (The dictionary defines "decent" as "marked by moral integrity."[4])

This kind of decency (gambling in some form) now exists in all but two American states—Hawaii and Utah. It's no wonder that a 2010 Gallup poll found only 12 percent of respondents gave state government officials a "very high/high" rating for honesty. Members of the U.S. Congress fared worse—only nine percent of respondents ranked their honesty as "very high/high" and 57 percent rated them "very low/low."[5]

Most people think the child sex-slave trade is only active in Southeast Asia, but it is alive and well in the United States. Las Vegas, Dallas, and Atlanta are major hubs of the child sex trade. Texas State Attorney Greg Abbot noted that the 2011 Super Bowl, held in Dallas, was "one of the biggest human trafficking events in the United States."[6]

In 2009, 7.2 million American adults were in jail, prison, or on parole, up from 1.7 million total in 1980.[7] Given these realities, it should come as no surprise that Gallup reported in January, 2011, only 30 percent of Americans expressed satisfaction with the current moral and ethical climate in the United States, marking a new low.[8] What's more, an astounding 76 percent of Americans say the moral condition of America is getting worse.[9] Had I been one of those polled in that survey I would have voted with the majority in both cases.

Too often, trends in the culture show up in the Church of Jesus Christ. And there is evidence that morality has fallen on hard times among God's people.

SHIFTING MORAL STANDARDS OF CHRISTIANS

The title of a study issued by the Barna Group says it all: "A New Generation of Adults Bends Moral and Sexual Rules to Their Liking." The report stated that attitudes of Christian believers born between 1965 and 1983 were "virtually identical" to the attitudes of non-believers in eight of the sixteen moral behaviors measured.[10] These included: gambling, pornography, abortion, sex outside of marriage, same-sex marriage and use of illegal drugs.[11] In a summary statement, David Kinnaman, the director of the study, wrote, "This research paints a compelling picture that moral values are shifting very quickly and significantly *within* the Christian community as well as outside of it."[12]

If those called to be salt and light in the world (Matthew 5:13-16) become those who need salt and light, what will happen to the world? The Christian's moral code is set firmly in Scripture and is all-encompassing, touching every facet of life. While there are not explicit guidelines for every aspect of modern life, there are principles from which decisions and choices can be deduced easily enough. For instance, Paul says in 1 Corinthians 10:31, ". . . do all to the glory of God." No Christian is justified in claiming ambiguity when it comes to moral issues. In any case, the adage "When in doubt, do without" applies until further insight is gained.

THE SOLID MORAL FOUNDATION FOR CHRISTIANS

God established a moral foundation for Israel in the Decalogue — the Ten Commandments (Exodus 20:1-17)—and additional laws. Jesus Christ then added a spiritual dimension to those laws in the Sermon on the Mount (Matthew 5-7). He then summarized all of God's laws with two: Love God (the first four commandments) and love your neighbor (the remaining six commandments). "On these two commandments hang all the Law and the Prophets" (Matthew 22:37-40).

For those Christians who believe living under grace means the absence of adhering to moral standards, there are four considerations:

Internalizing the Law

Through the prophet Jeremiah, God promised under the New Covenant to write His laws on the hearts of His people (Jeremiah 31:33) —the New Covenant being realized through faith in the crucified and resurrected Christ (Luke 22:20). Morality moves from being an external act of obedience to an internal motivation for righteousness. As the great Bible commentator Matthew Henry wrote, "When the law of God is written on our hearts, our duty will be our delight." And as Jesus said, ". . . My yoke is easy and My burden is light" (Matthew 11:30).

Affirming the Law

Paul clarifies that the law is good; that the law is established in the life of the Christian (Romans 3:31). Grace doesn't mean an absence of law; it means the power to keep God's laws willingly and cheerfully. And Paul affirms the two "love" commands of Jesus—love God and love neighbor—when he taught that love is the fulfillment of the law (Romans 13:8-10). Grace means living a moral life not because we have to but because we want to.

Sharpening the Law

Just because something is lawful doesn't automatically mean it's edifying: "All things are lawful for me, but not all things are helpful; all things are lawful for me, but not all things edify. Let no one seek his own, but each one the other's well-being" (1 Corinthians 10:23-24). The Christian Gospel of grace moves us to a higher plane in which we care more about others than we do about ourselves (1 Corinthians 10:24; Philippians 2:4). So we limit our actions—what might be lawful for us might be a stumbling block for another.

Honoring the Law

When a Christian acts immorally he negates the reason for the death of Christ on the cross: to satisfy the demands of the law (Ezekiel 18:4, 20; Galatians 3:13). Christ died and was raised from the dead in order that the *penalty* of the law might be paid and the *power* of sin might be broken (Romans 6:1-14; 8:1). Why would anyone who claims to have accepted God's gift of forgiveness for breaking the law choose to insult the Christ who procured that gift through His own suffering?

STRENGTH AND LIGHT BY THE LAW

In an ice-storm or windstorm it is always the trees with the deepest and strongest root systems that withstand the pressure to bend. It was God's intent for the nation of Israel to be like those hardwoods. His laws were designed to strengthen His people so they would not give in to the pressures of sin coming from the nations around them. If they obeyed God's laws they would be established high above all the nations of the earth (Deuteronomy 28.1). It was also Israel's calling to be a light to the Gentiles (Isaiah 49:6). And God's laws were to be a light to the world—the revelation of the character of God. But if Israel ignored God's law she would become as dark as the nations around her (Deuteronomy 28.50-07).

The Church is not the same as Israel, but we still have an obligation to reflect the moral character of God in order to be salt and light in the world (Matthew 5:13-14). The difference is that we don't follow or keep God's laws in order to attain moral standing with Him. Our righteousness is imputed to us by faith through the shared righteousness of Christ. He kept the law perfectly and gives us credit for doing so—while taking our sins upon Himself. But that grace doesn't mean we nullify the law. Rather, we uphold it (Romans 3:31).

Jesus said our righteousness must surpass the righteousness of the scribes and Pharisees (Matthew 5:20). They were focused on the letter of the law while ignoring the spirit of the law; they cleansed their hands but not their hearts (Matthew 23:27). They honored God with their lips while their hearts were far from Him (Isaiah 29:13). The point of Jesus' teaching in the Sermon on the Mount was to reveal the spirit of the law, to show us what God actually expects of us morally.

The warning to today's Church is this: Going through the motions of morality is not the morality God desires. Clean hands do not make a clean heart. But the opposite is true: Moral hearts will make moral hands. If we commit to keeping the spirit of the law, the letter of the law will, by default, be kept as well. And that is precisely the message Jesus delivered on a mountainside in Galilee.

THE SPIRIT OF GOD'S LAW

It's common for people today to believe God really doesn't expect them to keep a seemingly impossible standard of morality: telling the truth, keeping your word, staying married, being sexually pure, not harboring grudges, forgiving, and the like. Our modern cultures have learned to accept certain kinds of immoral behavior as normal—behaviors that would have been considered unthinkable in prior generations. That begs the question: What will the "new normal" morality be if we don't draw a line now?

Jesus addressed a similar situation in His day—a morality gap between what God expected (the law) and what religious leaders were willing to practice. In Matthew 5:21-47, He addressed six of those areas. He pointed out what the law said and explained what God really expects. And He concluded by saying, "Therefore, you shall be perfect, just as your Father in heaven is perfect" (verse 48). Perfect? Yes, perfection is God's standard. Man's inability to meet that standard opens the door for the Gospel of God's grace in Jesus Christ. What is impossible for man is possible for God. Jesus met God's standard of perfection for us.

The benefit of studying the six examples explained by Jesus is that they demonstrate how easy it is for humans to rationalize about morality; to take the path of least resistance; to do enough just to get by; to appear moral without having to do the hard work of self-discipline, self-denial, and sacrifice that is necessary to be truly moral and ethical. The point is that God expects more of us than we expect of ourselves. What passes for morality in America (and often in the Church) would get a failing grade in the kingdom of God.

The Meaning of Murder (Matthew 5:21-26)

The sixth commandment was clear in the physical sense: "You shall not murder" (Exodus 20:13). But are the feelings associated with murder (hate, revenge, envy) acceptable as long as we don't take the person's life? Jesus said no. Attacking a person with those motivations is another form of murder and is unacceptable in God's sight.

The Meaning of Adultery (Matthew 5:27-30)

Again, in the physical realm the Law was clear in the Ten Commandments: "You shall not commit adultery" (Exodus 20:14). But is committing physical adultery the only way to violate one's vows of purity in marriage? Jesus says there is a spiritual dimension to adultery that is just as immoral. When people engage in lust toward another, they betray their vows and disrespect their spouse and the object of their lust as well.

The Meaning of Divorce (Matthew 5:31-32)

Adjunct laws to the Ten Commandments provided for a bill of divorce as a form of legal protection for the wife against further exploitation by the divorcing husband (Deuteronomy 24:1-4). But Jesus wasn't interested in legal certificates. He said to divorce one's wife for any reason other than sexual impurity would turn her into an adulteress—an illegitimately divorced woman. He later said God only allowed divorces because of the hardness (sinfulness) of the human heart (Matthew 19:8).

The Meaning of Oaths (Matthew 5:33-37)

The Ten Commandments prohibited using God's name in vain (Exodus 20:7)—using God's name to validate a promise or oath. If the promise was then broken, God's name would have been used "in vain." Jesus put it simply: "But let your 'Yes' be 'Yes,' and your 'No,' 'No'." We should say what we mean and mean what we say.

The Meaning of Conflict (Matthew 5:38-42)

Laws of retribution in the Old Testament—"life shall be for life, eye for eye, tooth for tooth, hand for hand, foot for foot" (Deuteronomy 19:20-21)—were to limit acts of punishment, to keep a wronged person from extracting more than he lost. But Jesus amazed His listeners by saying it is better simply to settle conflicts quickly. If someone sues you, give them more than they ask for. In the kingdom, the focus is not on balancing the scales but on peace (Romans 12:21).

The Meaning of Enemies (Matthew 5:43-47)

The Old Testament Law said to "love your neighbor as yourself" (Leviticus 19:18b). But the Jewish scribes had added "and hate your enemy" to the verse and it became unofficial law because it seemed logical. But Jesus said love is for enemies as well as neighbors. And not just love for the sake of appearances, but true love from the heart.

Thankfully, One who is perfect has done what we are unable to do in our fallen strength. And He lives in all who belong to Him to move them toward the goal of being as perfect (blameless) as their Father in heaven.

Notes:

1. Pat Frode, "BYU puts principle over performance," *ESPN.com*, 2 March 2011, "http://sports.espn.go.com/espn/print?id=6175251&type=story#, accessed 3 March 2011.

2. http://sportsillustrated.cnn.com/vault/article/magazine/MAG1182621/index.htm, accessed 4-1-11.

3. Lesley Stahl, "Slot Machines: The Big Gamble," *60 Minutes*, 9 January 2011, http://www.cbsnews.com/video/watch/?id=7228424n&tag=contentMain;contentBody, accessed 23 February 2011.

4. *Merriam-Webster*, http://www.merriam-webster.com/dictionary/decent, accessed 10 May 2011.

5. Jeffery M. Jones, "Nurses Top Honesty and Ethics List for 11th Year," *Gallup.com*, 3 December 2010, http://www.gallup.com/poll/145043/Nurses-Top-Honesty-Ethics-List-11-Year.aspx, accessed 3 March 2011.

6. Katelyn Beaty, "Christians Launch Anti-Slavery Efforts for Super Bowl XLV," *blog. Christianity Today.com/women*, 25 January 2011, http://blog.christianitytoday.com/women/2011/01/christians_launch_antitraffick. html, accessed 25 January 2011.

7. U.S. Department of Justice figures. *http://bjs.ojp.usdoj.gov/content/glance/corr2.cfm*, accessed 4-3-11.

8. Jeffery M. Jones, "U.S. Satisfaction With Gov't, Morality, Economy Down Since '08," *Gallup.com*, 24 January 2011, http://www.gallup.com/poll/145760 Satisfaction-Gov-Morality-Economy-Down.aspx, accessed 25 January 2011.

9. Jeffery M. Jones, "American's Outlook for U.S. Morality Remains Bleak," *Gallup.com*, 17 May 2010, http://www.gallup.com/poll/128042/americans-outlook-morality-remains-bleak.aspx, accessed 3 March 2011.

10. "A New Generation of Adults Bends Moral and Sexual Rules to Their Liking," *Barna.org*, 31 October 2006, http://www.barna.org/barna-update/article/13-culture/144-a-new-generation-of-adults-bends-moral-and-sexual-rules-to-their-liking, accessed 31 October 2006.

11. Ibid.

12. Ibid. Emphasis in original.

APPLICATION

1. What principle does Paul express that helps in making decisions in the "gray" areas of life? (1 Corinthians 10:31)

   a. How does God's glory serve as a standard in making moral choices?

   b. How could God be hurt by a Christian making an immoral choice?

   c. How can faith serve as a helpful guide in making moral choices? (Romans 14:23)

   d. How does the variable of spiritual maturity figure in Romans 14:23? Is your faith as strong or wise today as it will be in a few years?

e. Why is, "When in doubt, do without" a good policy in moral decision making?

2. Read Romans 13:1-7.

a. What is moral when it comes to the laws of the land in which we live? (verse 1)

b. Who do we have to blame for being punished for breaking civil laws? (verse 2)

c. What is the purpose of civil authorities? (verse 4)

d. Ideally, whose laws should civil authorities be enforcing if they are "God's ministers"? (verses 4, 6)

e. What should a Christian do when immoral laws are enacted? (Consider laws allowing segregation, abortion, homosexuality, and others.)

f. In Peter's discussion on the same subject, what admonition does he give about how to live? (1 Peter 2:15-16)

g. How is 1 Peter 2:17 a good overview and guide for moral living? How does "fear God" mirror 1 Corinthians 10:31?

3. Read Matthew 22:37-40.

a. Jesus' most important commandment is: (verse 37)

b. Jesus' second-most important commandment is: (verse 39)

c. How will perfect love toward the three people Jesus' mentions—God, neighbor, self—preclude any immoral acts?

d. Does all immorality flow from a lack of love? Explain.

e. How does Paul's message in Romans 13:8-10 support the idea that love is the fulfillment of the law?

f. How does 1 John 4:18 support the primacy of love in moral decision making?

DID YOU KNOW?

L ex talionis—the law of retaliation—is expressed three times in the Old Testament: Exodus 21:23-25; Leviticus 24:17-22; Deuteronomy 19:20-21. It is important to note that it was not meant to be interpreted literally in every case. Rather, it expressed a principle of just compensation or retribution for an aggrieved party. The Law was expressed as life for life, eye for eye, tooth for tooth, hand for hand, or foot for foot. The loss of a body part was not so common that laws were set to regulate compensation. Rather, these examples serve to illustrate the principle of balanced judgment. Even in the case of a capital crime in which capital punishment was mandated ("life for life"), mitigating factors came into play (Exodus 21:12, 14, 19, 21, 26-28, 30).

...WHEN THE BIBLE WOULD BE MARGINALIZED

Selected Scriptures

In this lesson we learn about the growing marginalization of the Bible in American culture and churches.

OUTLINE

Biblical literacy was at its highest in America in the first century after the nation's founding—and it has been decreasing ever since. Slowly but surely, the Bible has been pushed to the periphery of the public square. And as often happens, as goes the nation so goes the church.

I. **The Marginalization of the Bible**

II. **The Meaning of Marginalization**

III. **Modern, Marginal Christians**
   A. The Example of Leaders and Authorities
   B. The Price of Loyalty
   C. The Fear of Shame
   D. The Fear of Offense
   E. The Fear of Competition

IV. **Measuring Marginalization**

A: In Adam's Fall we sinned all.

B: Heaven to find, the Bible mind.

C: Christ crucify'd for sinners dy'd.

D: The Deluge drown'd the Earth around.

E: Elijah hid by Ravens fed.

. . . and so on through the remainder of the alphabet.

If you had lived near the end of the seventeenth century in America, you likely would have learned your ABC's in the above form from *The New England Primer*. From that same book you would have taught your children to pray, "Now I lay me down to sleep, I pray the Lord my soul to keep . . ."

The New England Primer was "the single most influential Christian textbook in history. Most scholars agree that most, if not all, of the [American] Founding Fathers were taught to read and write using this volume which is unsurpassed to this day for its excellence of practical training and Christian worldview. First published in 1690, the goal of the *Primer* was to combine the study of the Bible with the alphabet, vocabulary, and the reading of prose and poetry. . ."[1]

The *Primer* was gradually replaced by *McGuffey's Readers*, a series of biblically-influenced reading books written by William McGuffey. Four volumes of *McGuffey's Readers* were published in 1837, with McGuffey's brother adding two more volumes in the 1840s. William McGuffey's Presbyterian Calvinism permeated these readers from which millions of children learned to read in the nineteenth century.

When McGuffey died in 1873 his *Readers* were made totally secular—all references to the Bible and God and a biblical worldview were removed:

"The revised *Readers* were compiled to meet the needs of national unity and the dream of an American melting pot for the world's oppressed masses. The Calvinist values of salvation, righteousness, and piety, so prominent in the early *Readers*, were excluded from the later versions. The content of the books was secularized and replaced by middle-class civil religion, morality, and values. McGuffey's name was featured on these revised editions, yet he neither contributed to them nor approved their content."[2]

Do you see the trend in American education? In the eighteenth century, *The New England Primer* was *explicitly* biblical. In the nineteenth century, the original *McGuffey's Readers* were *implicitly* biblical. In the late nineteenth and early twentieth century, the revised *McGuffey's Readers* were *wholly secular*. And then came modern, twentieth-century education under the influence of John Dewey, the father of progressive American education.

John Dewey (1859-1952) was a psychologist and philosopher who is most responsible for how American children are educated today. He changed the priority in education from acquiring knowledge to experiencing knowledge:

> "In the 1920s/1930s, John Dewey became famous for pointing out that the authoritarian, strict, pre-ordained knowledge approach of modern traditional education was too concerned with delivering knowledge, and not enough with understanding students' actual experiences."[3]

John Dewey changed American education from the didactic transfer of knowledge based on a biblical worldview beginning in the late 1600's to the modern view that experience is what drives the acquisition of knowledge. Yet God said in Hosea 4:6, "My people are destroyed for lack of knowledge." In Deuteronomy 6:4-9 God lays out a pattern for delivering knowledge: It should be communicated as part of the course of life. And Jesus condemned the scribes and Pharisees for taking away "the key of knowledge" (Luke 11:52).

From God's perspective, knowledge was not so much about *discovering* truth as being *conformed* to truth as set forth in the Book of Proverbs: "The fear of the Lord is the beginning of knowledge, but fools despise wisdom and instruction" (1:7). The Puritan settlers in America brought this perspective with them. In his last sermon to the congregation leaving from his church in Holland in 1620, pastor John Robinson exhorted them, when they arrived in America, to follow the Lord Jesus Christ and His Word: "I am verily persuaded that the Lord yet has more truth to break forth from His holy Word."[4] The wisdom they would need in the new world would not "break forth" from their experience but from God's Word.

THE MARGINALIZATION OF THE BIBLE

Sadly, the objective knowledge of God's Word has slowly been diluted, and in many cases disappeared altogether, from the American landscape. We now have public schools that are patrolled by armed security guards, and students who are adrift morally and significantly behind their international peers in academic proficiency. Instead of the Bible being used as a textbook or sourcebook in education, now it is banned. In our journey from Plymouth to Pluralism, the Bible has been downgraded from taught to tolerated in the public square —and barely tolerated, at that. From being a rule of faith and practice, the Bible has become a relic of history; a cultural icon used to illustrate the narrow-mindedness of those who founded the nation.

And as much as I hate to admit it, the public square is not the only venue in which the Bible's status has been downgraded and its message diluted. It's also happening in the last place we should expect it: in the Christian Church itself.

This lesson is not about the Bible's marginalization in public venues but in the Church of Jesus Christ. I cite those public realities to make this point: *As goes the culture, (too often) so goes the Church.* The Bible no longer has pride of place in many American churches. Too many pulpits are focused on *experiential* knowledge instead of *propositional* knowledge. In short, the Bible has been marginalized in American culture and is in danger of being marginalized in the Church.

THE MEANING OF MARGINALIZATION

Marginalization means to push something to the periphery or outer edge of significance. And it happens slowly over time. Christian and other books were outright banned and burned in Nazi Germany in 1933, which is different from marginalization. When something is marginalized, its influence is reduced without it being totally removed. And that is what is happening to the Bible in American culture and in many churches.

How can a majority of Americans profess to be Christians while the sourcebook for their religion is being marginalized? It's because they don't realize that the Bible is a living book that is indispensable to a living faith. They believe it is possible to be a Christian without knowing and applying God's truth which is found only in Scripture.

MODERN, MARGINAL CHRISTIANS

In 1521, England's William Tyndale told a local clergyman that his goal was for a plowboy to know more Scripture than the clergyman—a task that seemed impossible since the Bible wasn't available to the common man in English at the time.[5] The Bible was available only in Latin, a language able to be read only by priests (if by them). (In 1519, Catholic officials in England put to death a woman and six men for having taught their children English versions of the Lord's Prayer, the Ten Commandments, and the Apostles' Creed!)[6]

Tyndale, fluent in eight languages, fled persecution in England and continued his work in Europe. He completed the New Testament in English and parts of the Old Testament but was apprehended—imprisoned, strangled, and burned at the stake—in 1536. By 1539, King Henry VIII required that English Bibles be available to all English-speaking parishioners. So Tyndale's goal was realized even though not in his lifetime.

Many since Tyndale have given their lives for the sake of putting the Bible into the hands of people around the world. Yet many today will not fight to keep the Bible from being marginalized in their culture and their church—for several reasons.

The Example of Leaders and Authorities

For the first hundred years or so it was easy to be a Christian in America. Most leaders, if not professing Christians, had a high regard for the truths of the Bible pertaining to morals and ethics. The Bible was quoted in the halls of government and education—it was part of the cultural conversation. Citizens followed their leaders' example of respect, if not reverence, for the Bible. But times have changed. Leaders are marginalizing the Bible and citizens are following their example.

In the two primary New Testament passages on Christians and government (Romans 13:1-7; 1 Peter 2:13-17) there is no indication that civil leaders have been given stewardship over God's Word. It was Scottish Presbyterian theologian Samuel Rutherford who, in his 1644 book *Lex, Rex: or The Law and the Prince*, clarified the Christian's relationship to government: Where government's laws conform to God's laws, governments are to be obeyed. When government's laws conflict with God's laws, the latter always takes precedent [7]

If civil authorities marginalize the Word of God it is up to Christians to elevate it in the culture. It is easy to be lulled into complacency by the example of leaders.

The Price of Loyalty

Christians in America may not pay with their life like William Tyndale did for promoting the reading of God's Word, but there are other prices to pay. A story from the Old Testament illustrates:

King Ahab once said he hated the prophet Micaiah "because he does not prophesy good concerning me, but evil" (1 Kings 22:8). The king hated the prophet because the prophet lived by this rule: "As the Lord lives, whatever the Lord says to me, that I will speak" (verse 14). When Micaiah prophesied that Ahab would suffer a military defeat, the prophet was put in prison and given nothing but bread and water. Those who are loyal to the Word of God pay a price. (Micaiah was right: Ahab was killed in battle.)

Christians in the community or in school may pay a price for promoting biblical values. A Christian legislator may be ridiculed for quoting the Bible in the halls of government. For some people, the price is too high. They will not run the risk of punishment or persecution or ridicule as the price for remaining loyal to God's Word.

The Fear of Shame

There can be a physical cost, or a cost to one's reputation, for loyalty to the Bible. But one can be made to feel ashamed for believing the Bible as well. Nowhere is this seen more clearly than in the efforts of the "New Atheists." This group of intellectuals has released a spate of books in the last few years ridiculing religion and Christianity in particular. They believe "religion should not simply be tolerated but should be countered, criticized and exposed by rational argument whenever its influence arises."[8] Christians are being made to feel foolish by the attacks of those like the New Atheists.

The apostle Peter said that we should "always be ready to give a defense to everyone who asks [us] a reason for the hope that is in [us]" (1 Peter 3:15). But one of the most intellectual Christian theologians who ever lived, Karl Barth, put it this way: "Jesus loves me, this I know, for the Bible tells me so."[9] That was his summary of the millions of words he wrote in his 13-volume *Church Dogmatics*. The apostle Paul carefully explained why no one, in his day or in ours, should be intimidated or ashamed by those who use intellectual prowess to marginalize God and His Word (1 Corinthians 1:18-2:16).

The Fear of Offense

America's newest religion must be the religion of tolerance which says that all religions are worthy of respect. No problem there—it's the reason they believe all religions are equally respectable that is the problem: There is no such thing as ultimate truth, so every religion's version of truth is equally valid.

But Jesus said, "I am the way, the truth, and the life. No one comes to the Father except through Me" (John 14:6). Because of embracing these words of Jesus, Christians are called intolerant while at the same time being the least tolerated. As long as you don't offend anyone in modern society by saying your religion is "the only way" you will be tolerated. But the Bible says that offense is inevitable in this world, that the Gospel will be a stumbling stone to many: "a stone to trip over, a boulder blocking the way" (1 Peter 2:6-8). For many, the message of the cross of Christ is "foolishness" (or offensive) (1 Corinthians 1:18).

Being afraid to allow the Gospel to offend those who may stumble over it is how the Bible gets marginalized in our day. We cannot be afraid of how some will respond to the message of Christianity.

The Fear of Competition

Many churches compete for attendance and revenue which leads them to co-opt the modern values of the entertainment industry. They use the world's marketing and entertainment techniques to attract and hold new members. And ultimately, that leads to the devolution of the church in such a setting. It's hard for the Bible to compete for time and place in a one-hour "worship" service that is based on entertainment.

As the senior pastor of a large church I recognize the thin line that exists between biblical and worldly life in the church. And I should not (and will not) try to impose the values of my church on any other. All I can do is remind myself and others that as the world goes, (too often) so goes the church. As the seasoned pastor and leader Chuck Swindoll has pointed out, when a church has more people on its media staff than its pastoral staff, or when more of the budget is spent on media than on shepherding, "something is out of whack."[10]

The first thing mentioned in a list of the early Church's priorities is a devotion to "the apostles' doctrine" (Acts 2:42). And we have no license from God to change that priority today.

MEASURING MARGINALIZATION

Research by organizations like Barna, Gallup, and Pew reveals a discouraging picture of how Americans view the Bible—even professing Christians—based on how they interact with the Bible in their personal lives. For instance, in 2006 the Gallup organization asked people whether the Bible is the inspired Word of God to be taken literally, or not. Only 26 percent of those polled said "Yes"— down from 40 percent in 1980. The number of people saying the Bible is a collection of stories, fables, myths, history, and teachings increased from 10 percent in 1980 to 19 percent in 2006.[11] Based on other research, we have to assume that between 75-85 percent of the respondents were professing Christians.

The Barna Group found that 90 percent of those aged 64+ see the Bible as a holy book, while only 67 percent of those 18-25 hold the same view. Comparing the Bible, Quran, and Book of Mormon, 43 percent of respondents believe all three books "offer the same spiritual truths."[12]

You and I have no control over how others view or treat the Bible. But there is one place we can stop its marginalization: in our own lives. When we do that, the Bible will gain new traction in our homes, churches, communities, and yes—even our nation.

Notes:

1. "Publisher's Note," *The New-England Primer: Improved for the More Easy Attaining the True Reading of English. To Which Is Added the Assembly of Divines, and Mr. Cotton's Catechism* (Boston, 1777; reprint by The Vision Forum, Inc., 2002-2010).

2. "McGuffey Readers," wikipedia.com. http://en.wikipedia.org/wiki/McGuffey%27s_Readers, accessed 3-18-11.

3. http://wilderdom.com/experiential/ExperientialDewey.html

4. *Works of John Robinson* (London: John Snow, 1851), xliv.

5. Tony Lane, "A Man for All People: Introducing William Tyndale." *Christian History*, Vol. VI, No. 4, Issue 16, 7.

6. "Did You Know . . .?", *Christian History*, Vol. VI, No. 4, Issue 16, 4.

7. Rutherford's work was updated for the modern church by the late theologian Francis A. Schaeffer in his book *A Christian Manifesto* (Crossway Books, 1981, 1982).

8. http://articles.cnn.com/2006-11-08/world/atheism.feature_1_new-atheists-new-atheism-religion?_s=PM:WORLD, accessed 3-22-11.

9. http://www.gci.org/history/barth, accessed 3-22-11.

10. Chuck Swindoll, "The Problem with Pizzazz." LeadershipJournal.net, May 2, 2011. http://www.christianitytoday.com/le/2011/spring/problempizzazz.html (accessed 5-24-11)

11. http://www.gallup.com/video/22864/Biblical-Beliefs.aspx, accessed 3-20-11.

12. "New Research Explores How Different Generations View and Use the Bible," *Barna Group*, 19 October 2009, http://www.barna.org/barna-update/article/12-faithspirituality/317-new-research-explores-how-different-generations-view-and-use-the-bible

1. Read Hosea 4:1, 6

   a. In addition to truth and mercy, what did God say was missing in the nation of Israel? (verse 1)

   b. How critical was the absence of knowledge in the land? (verse 6a)

   c. What did God reject in Israel when the people rejected knowledge of Him? (verse 6b)

   d. With what did God equate knowledge? What was the knowledge the people rejected? (verse 6c)

2. Read Deuteronomy 6:6-9.

   a. What were the words Moses referred to in verse 6? (see verses 1-3)

b. In what kinds of settings were parents to teach these words to their children? (verse 7)

c. What are the implications of the word "diligently" in verse 7?

d. Verse 7 contains two figures of speech called "merism"—the citing of opposite extremes (sitting vs. walking; lying down vs. rising up). What is being communicated about when and where to communicate God's Word to one's children?

e. What was symbolized by the Jews tying copies of the Word around the forehead or on their hand? (verse 8)

f. What was accomplished by writing portions of the Word on the doorposts and gates of one's house? (verse 9)

g. What is the "big idea" of this passage about the Word of God in the life of the Jews?

3. What is the theme of Luke 11:37-52? (See verses 42, 43, 44, 46, 47, 52.)

a. What is the last "woe" Jesus pronounces on the Pharisees? (verse 52)

b. What is the "key of knowledge"? (verse 52)

c. How did the Pharisees take it away from the people? (See Amos 8:11 for a clue.)

4. What does Proverbs 1:7 say is the "beginning of knowledge"?

a. What does a fool do with knowledge of God when he receives it? (verse 7b)

b. What does the Word of God make one wise to do? (2 Timothy 3:15)

c. And what four practical dimensions does it bring to the one who embraces it? (2 Timothy 3:16)

DID YOU KNOW?

The collection of writings—66 books—that make up the Protestant Bible are often referred to as the "canon" of Scripture. "Canon" comes from a Semitic word (*qaneh*) that meant "reed" —or a stiff stalk that was used as a measuring device. In the biblical sense, therefore, the canon of Scripture refers to the books that have passed the chief measure of inclusion: divine inspiration. Both the Protestant and Jewish Old Testaments contain 39 books. The Roman Catholic and Orthodox canons add additional books to the Old Testament known as the Apocrypha (Greek for "hidden" or "obscure"). While Protestant scholars have found many of the Apocryphal books to be edifying reading (like Wisdom of Solomon) and helpful in historical studies (like 1 and 2 Maccabees), they were never recognized as inspired by Protestant church councils.

...WHEN THE CHURCH WOULD BE IRRELEVANT

Selected Scriptures

In this lesson we will explore the claim that the Christian Church has become irrelevant in modern America.

OUTLINE

America was built on a biblical base. After all, the Puritans who were among the first settlers came seeking religious freedom. The church was the most relevant institution in America's early years but some wonder whether she has lost her influence. It is up to the church to decide.

I. Discussing the Reality of the Church

II. Determining the Relevancy of the Church

III. Defining the Role of the Church
    A. The Church's Purpose: The Glory of God
    B. The Church's Priority: The Great Commission
    C. The Church's Program: The Great Commandment

The son of a friend of mine recently attended a wedding, held in a barn, where the female minister made this pronouncement: "And now, by the authority vested in me by the World Wide Web, I pronounce you husband and wife." Her comments produced giggles in the service and questions at the reception: "How does the Internet give one authority to conduct weddings?" It turns out she received her ministerial license from an online school of some sort. Laughable, yet legal in the eyes of the law.

That's an example of how the church has changed in recent years. It has moved from being a relevant, center-of-community institution to one that is increasingly irrelevant (in the eyes of many) and on the edge of the community. The place where the community used to gather for weddings, funerals, town meetings, and celebrations is now being viewed as old-fashioned and outdated. Society views the Christian church as just another option in an endless menu of choices for opinions, inspiration, services, and entertainment.

Sometimes people try to find their way into the church but find the welcome mat missing. That happened to famous Dutch painter Vincent van Gogh (1853-1890) as a young man. Sensing a call to serve God in pastoral or missionary ministry, he could not convince local church authorities to accept him. So he stopped trying and withdrew from church involvement—except in two of his most famous paintings. *Starry Night* pictures a village in a valley at night with warm lights glowing in the windows of many houses, and bright swirls of light in the heavens. But the village church is shrouded in darkness, seemingly devoid of life. *The Church at Auvers* presents a daytime scene of the town church that has no doors—at least none are visible. People on the outside can't get in; people on the inside don't go out. The road approaching the church splits into a "Y" and bypasses the church on either side, as if to say that the life of the town goes by the church but never to the church.

Van Gogh was no doubt expressing his personal frustrations with the church: dark, devoid of light and life, no way to get in or out, the life of the world passing the church and never bothering to stop. The artist left no written records of why he painted the churches the way he did. But we have to assume it was due to his own negative experiences as a young man.

Van Gogh's paintings beg the question, "How would the American church in 2011 be painted? What kind of image does it reflect to the world?" I worry that the church in our day is trying so hard to make herself relevant that she is becoming irrelevant! We are majoring in entertainment and experience which means we're competing with Hollywood, sports, and endless media. And that is not a competition we will win—nor should we. When the church loses her one distinctive voice—the voice of Scripture inviting people to be reconciled to God through faith in Christ—then we find ourselves competing with all the other voices in the marketplace.

No one else in the world has the Church's message—the Gospel of Jesus Christ. That message is what makes us relevant. If we lose that message, we lose our relevance. I agree with these thoughts from my friend Chuck Swindoll:

> Some time ago a group of church leaders decided that they didn't want to be hated. They focused just on attracting more and more people. But if we're here to offer something the world can't provide, why would I want to copy the world? There is plenty of television. There are plenty of talk shows. There are plenty of comedians. But there is not plenty of worship of the true and living God . . .
>
> Here's what troubles me: I don't know why leaders younger than me aren't saying this. I'm not talking about novices, but the leaders in their forties and fifties. Why aren't they raising questions and showing some concern for where the church is heading with its focus on media and headcount and passive spectating? I know one church that has 17 people on their media staff and only 12 on the pastoral staff.
>
> When a church is spending more of its budget on media than shepherding, something is out of whack.[1]

As a pastor of a large church I know how challenging it is to maintain a biblical focus and not be seduced by the methods, messages, and marketing of the world. It's a constant struggle to define relevance biblically instead of by the world's standards. I never thought I'd see the day when the Church of Jesus Christ was looked on as irrelevant. But that day has arrived—and I think the church has to assume some of the blame. If the church is being ignored because we preach the message of "Jesus Christ and Him crucified" (1 Corinthians 2:2), or because the Gospel has become "a stumbling stone and rock of offense" (Romans 9:33), that's one thing. But if we are deemed irrelevant because we're an anemic version of the world's entertainment options—because we aren't playing the world's game as well as the world does—then that's another.

If we're going to be attacked or ignored by the world, it might as well be for "[turning] the world upside down" like the early Church did (Acts 17:6).

DISCUSSING THE REALITY OF THE CHURCH

The word "church" has become confusing. In the New Testament it never refers to a building where Christians meet; it always refers to the universal body of believers in Christ. The Greek word *ekklesia* meant "called out ones"—those called out of the world by God to form the Body of Christ. The great English Bible translator Tyndale used the English word "congregation" to refer to groups of Christians instead of "church"—a good distinction that didn't stick.

Today, "church" refers to both people and buildings; obviously, the spiritual organism of the Church is most important. Jesus didn't send a building into the world to preach the Gospel, He sent people (Matthew 28:19-20; Acts 1:8). So if the Church is losing her relevance in the world it is not because of our buildings. There is only one place to look to discover the reason: in the mirror.

I am not anti-church building by any means. All the benefits that accrue to a nuclear family from having a physical structure to call home accrue to church families as well. The "Church gathered" is the flip side of the "Church scattered." Both are important, and church buildings allow the Church to gather for worship (celebration) and for instruction and fellowship (congregation), while discipleship and accountability are best accomplished in the "scattered" mode (cells).

The point is to maintain a clear understanding of the difference between Church and church—and the priority of the former over the latter. Church buildings can necessitate huge investments of resources for construction and maintenance, and they are only temporary. Keeping the focus on people is the biblical priority and will result in the Church remaining relevant.

DETERMINING THE RELEVANCY OF THE CHURCH

The Barna Group compiled survey results in 2010 from a cross-section of Americans and their opinions about "the Church"—and the results were not encouraging.[2] Positively, 19 percent of respondents noted the church's efforts to help the needy. But 25 percent could not name a single positive contribution made by the church in recent years.

And 25 percent also cited violence or hatred being spread in the name of Christ. It's sad that one-fourth of those surveyed have that perception. No doubt part of it arises due to the Church's general position on issues like homosexuality and abortion and other moral matters. But there are some instances where the church has blackened its own eye: clergy sexual abuse of children, other moral failures by church leaders, and focus on wealth and materialism. We deserve whatever criticism accrues from these failures on our part.

There are numerous written records from the early centuries of the Church in the ancient world—their positive impact and humble lifestyles and their beneficial effect on their communities. Rodney Stark, a modern scholar who has written extensively about early and modern Christianity, says this about the relevance of the Church in its early years:

"Christianity revitalized life in Greco-Roman cities by providing new norms and new kinds of social relationships able to cope with many urgent problems. To cities filled with the homeless and impoverished, Christianity offered charity as well as hope. To cities filled with newcomers and strangers, Christianity offered an immediate basis for attachment. To cities filled with orphans and widows, Christianity provided a new and expanded sense of family. To cities torn by violent ethnic strife, Christianity offered a new basis for social solidarity. And to cities faced with epidemics, fire, and earthquakes, Christianity offered effective nursing services . . . For what they brought was not simply an urban movement, but a new culture capable of making life in Greco-Roman cities more tolerable."[3]

At the very least, we can say that the Church *has been* relevant. Unfortunately, biblical Christianity is no longer being preached from every pulpit in the land. As a result, America is losing her spiritual way, and it is due, in no small part, to the fact that the Church has lost her way.

DEFINING THE ROLE OF THE CHURCH

I am hopeful that the Church can once again become salt and light in our nation if she will re-commit to focusing on the roles God has given her. The value of the Church can be measured by three vital dimensions, which combine to make it relevant to society —indeed not only relevant, but absolutely crucial to society's continuation. To understand the Church's value to the world, let's examine these three dimensions one by one.

The Church's Purpose: The Glory of God

No one really knows who first topped a church building with a steeple, but the practice dates back about fourteen hundred years to when churches had clock towers and bell turrets, which were often the tallest structures in town.

I love steeples because they point toward the heavens and direct the eye upward to our risen Savior. Preachers come and go. Songs become popular and fade into forgetfulness. Trends and methods change with the years. But throughout all these changes, church steeples have remained a constant tradition. I am thankful that those aspiring spires still point toward the heavens because they are fitting reminders of where the Church's focus should be.

But I also love steeples because they get smaller as they get closer to heaven, which is what happens to all of us as we grow closer to the Lord. The closer we get to Him, the more we realize that the lesson of the steeple is that the Church's purpose is to glorify God!

The Church's Priority: The Great Commission

There is nothing more relevant to each and every soul in the universe than the good news of Jesus Christ. A relevant Church must be carried along by the fresh winds of the Great Commission. At the end of Matthew's Gospel, Jesus tells us to go into all the world, winning, baptizing, teaching, and making disciples in all nations (Matthew 28:18–20). At the beginning of Acts, He says to His followers, "You shall receive power when the Holy Spirit has come upon you; and you shall be witnesses to Me . . . to the end of the earth" (1:8).

The Lord Jesus promised to build His Church, and the gates of hell cannot prevent it (Matthew 16:18). Even if the Church is reduced to a tiny, persecuted, ridiculed minority in the Western world, she can confidently pursue the priority her Savior has given her. Whether we're respected in society or neglected and abused, we have a mission—to take the good news of Christ to the ends of the earth and to bring the Gospel within earshot of anyone willing to listen. We aren't here to be successful, influential, wealthy, famous, or praised by a degraded society. We're here to pave the way for the Lord's return by sowing the Gospel, both person-to-person and nation-to-nation.

The Great Commission is to go into all the world and preach the Gospel to every creature. God left us here with a message, and that message is the Gospel of Jesus Christ.

The Church's Program: The Great Commandment

The Great Commandment is found in Matthew 22 where we read that we're to love our neighbor as ourelves (v. 39). Our ministry of compassion is one aspect of our faith that critics cannot deny. The world respects our historic concern for the poor, the innocent, the downtrodden, the sick, the underprivileged, the orphans, the widows, and the needy. The pundits may rail against our stand on immorality, but they respect our help for the homeless. The Bible says, "Live such good lives among the pagans that, though they accuse you of doing wrong, they may see your *good deeds* and glorify God" (1 Peter 2:12 NIV, emphasis mine here and in the following verses).

Jesus said, "Let your light so shine before men, that they may see your *good works* and glorify your Father in heaven" (Matthew 5:16). Paul said that we have been "created in Christ Jesus for *good works*, which God prepared" for us to do (Ephesians 2:10).

We're to be like Dorcas, who "was full of *good works* and charitable deeds which she did" (Acts 9:36). We're commanded to be rich in *good works*, prepared for every *good work*, equipped for every *good work*, zealous for *good works*, and in all things showing ourselves to be a pattern of *good works* (1 Timothy 6:18; 2 Timothy 2:21; 3:17; Titus 2:14; 2:7).

The good deed you or I do for someone authenticates our testimony, shares the compassion of our Lord, and paves the way for our message. May God grant His Church the discipline to stay focused and the desire to manifest the eternal relevance of Jesus Christ to a needy world.

Notes:

1. Chuck Swindoll, "The Problem with Pizzazz," LeadershipJournal.net, May 2, 2011. http://www.christianity today.com/le/2011/spring/problem/pizzazz.html, accessed 5-23-11.

2. "Americans Say Serving the Needy Is Christianity's Biggest Contribution to Society," October 25, 2010, The Barna Group. http://www.barna.org/faith-spirituality/440-americans-describe-christianity-contributions,accessed 4-8-11.

3. Rodney Stark, *The Rise of Christianity: How the Obscure, Marginal, Jesus Movement Became the Dominant Religious Force in the Western World in a Few Centuries* (New York: HarperOne, 1997), 161-162.

1. Read Matthew 16:13-20.

    a. What was the subject of Jesus' discussion with His disciples? (verse 13)

    b. What answer did Peter give that gained Jesus' approval? (verse 16)

    c. Peter's name (*petros*) meant "stone," whereas "rock" (*petra*) meant "bedrock." What "bedrock" was Jesus referring to in verse 18 upon which He would build His Church?

    d. If Jesus were referring to Peter's confession (verse 16) as the foundation of the Church, how does that help define the Church's mission?

e. How does the Great Commission (Matthew 28:19-20) support verse 16 as the focus and priority of the Church?

f. Whose responsibility is it to "build" Christ's Church? (verse 18)

g. How do churches at times act like it is up to them to build and expand the Church?

h. What happens when members of the church assume responsibilities that belong solely to the Head of the Church?

i. What do you believe are the several key priorities that, when practiced, would result in Christ's Church being built?

2. Read Acts 2:42-47.

   a. What do you find in verse 47a that indicates the Jerusalem church was seen as relevant by the people in the city?

   b. What connection is there between people (non-Christians) joining churches and the church's relevance? (verse 47b) (Do people join groups they consider irrelevant?)

   c. What four activities seem to have dominated the life of the Jerusalem church? (verse 42)

      1. The apostles _____.

      2. _____.

      3. The breaking of _____.

      4. _____.

d. Besides miracles, what signs of God's presence might convey a sense of relevance in today's culture? (verse 43)

e. What message was likely communicated by their sharing? (verses 44-45)

f. What do "temple" and "house to house" communicate about the different venues of their church life? (verse 46a)

g. Why would modern people find "gladness and simplicity of heart" to be very appealing? (verse 46b)

The Hartford Institute for Religion Research estimates there are around 335,000 religious congregations meeting in America today. Roughly 300,000 are Protestant and other Christian groups, 22,000 are Catholic and Orthodox, and 12,000 non-Christian congregations. The median church in the U.S. has 75 participants in Sunday morning services (median = the point where half are larger and half are smaller), but the average church has 186 participants due to the influence of mega churches on the average. Small churches draw only 11 percent of those attending on Sunday while 50 percent of churchgoers attend the largest 10 percent of congregations (those with 350 or more participants). From the Hartford Institute for Religious Research "Fast Facts." http://hirr.hartsem.edu/research/fastfacts/fast_facts.html,accessed 6-7-11.

...WHEN A MUSLIM STATE COULD INTIMIDATE THE WORLD

Selected Scriptures

In this lesson we learn about a Muslim-dominated country that is becoming a threat to the stability of the Middle East and the world.

OUTLINE

Religiously, Iran is home to predominantly Shia Muslims and is controlled by the chief Muslim cleric. Iran is a theocracy—a government informed by religious beliefs. Her religious leaders view Iran as chosen by Allah to usher in Muslim rule over all the earth.

I. **Iran: A Theocratic Threat to the World**
    A. Awaiting Her Messiah
    B. Angry With America
    C. A Plan for Israel
    D. Ahmadinejad and the Clerics

II. **Iran: A Transition to Militancy**
    A. From the Shah to the Ayatollahs
    B. From Clerics to a Crisis

III. **Iran: From Friend to Foe to Fanatic**
    A. A Former Friend of Israel
    B. A Foe of the International Community
    C. A Fanatic to Be Watched

"In the name of God, the Compassionate, the Merciful. All praise be to Allah, the Lord of the Universe, and peace and blessing be upon our Master and Prophet, Muhammad, and his pure Household, and his noble Companions and on all divine messengers. Oh, God, hasten the arrival of Imam Al-Mahdi and grant him good health and victory and make us his followers and those who attest to his rightfulness."[1]

If you think that is a prayer offered in a Muslim synagogue somewhere in the world, you are wrong. It was offered at the United Nations before the sixty-fifth session of the General Assembly on September 23, 2010. The "pray-er"? Iranian President Mahmoud Ahmadinejad. Did you hear anything about this prayer being offered? Probably not.

This lesson is about the ancient nation of Iran (Persia) intimidating the rest of the world, something I never thought I would see. Iran is a theocracy—a government informed by religion. In Iran's case, the god is Allah, the Muslim god. Because it is a theocracy, the chief Muslim cleric in Iran is the true leader of the nation while Ahmadinejad is the public and political head of the nation. Other national bullies in modern history—Hitler, Mussolini, Stalin, Mao—have not based their aggressiveness on religious beliefs like Iran has. And that's what makes Iran so dangerous. A nation with nuclear weapon capability that believes it is on a mission from God is a new threat on the world stage.

Religious commitment is to be commended. But when its weapons are fear, threats, and intimidation instead of love and righteousness (John 13:35), it is time to be concerned. Jesus will one day establish a theocratic kingdom on earth (Revelation 20:1-6), but it will be based on justice and righteousness.

IRAN: A THEOCRATIC THREAT TO THE WORLD

Let's look again at the prayer Ahmadinejad prayed at the United Nations and unpack the theology hidden in it.

Awaiting Her Messiah

Just as Christians await the return of the Lord Jesus Christ to earth to establish His kingdom, so Shia Muslims await their own messiah, called Al-Mahdi, or the twelfth imam—the twelfth religious leader of Islam in direct succession from the prophet Muhammad, the founder of Islam. Shia Muslims comprise 85-90 percent of the Muslim population of Iran. They believe Al-Mahdi was born in A.D. 869 and never died; he has been in hiding and will be revealed as the savior of mankind at the right time. Iran's leaders believe Al-Mahdi will return to Iran as his host nation and that Iran will play the key national role in "the administration of the world" after his return.[2]

Angry With America

Shia Muslims believe Al-Mahdi will return at a time of great chaos. Therefore, it is to their advantage to create such chaos to hasten his return! Iran believes the United States knows this and is doing whatever it can to suppress Iran's rise to leadership in the Middle East, to keep Al-Mahdi from revealing himself to Iran. Ahmadinejad has said the U.S. is trying "to prevent the coming of the Hidden Imam because they know that the Iranian nation is the one that will prepare the grounds for his coming and will be the supporters of his rule."[3]

A Plan for Israel

Ahmadinejad has also declared, more than once, that Israel should be "wiped out from the map" of the Middle East.[4] This rhetoric has intensified in recent months due to speculation about whether Israel will try to knock out Iran's nuclear capability. In May, 2010, Ahmadinejad's chief of staff said that such an attack on Iran would result in Israel's destruction in less than ten days.[5]

To summarize: Iran believes it is the preeminent Muslim nation of the world, the nation to which the Muslim messiah will return. Iran also believes that the U.S. is its enemy and that Israel has no right to exist in the Middle East. And all of these views are fueled by religious fanaticism—and funded by the third largest proven oil reserves in the world. Iran is not a toothless tiger.

Ahmadinejad and the Clerics

As stated, Ahmadinejad is simply the public mouthpiece of the radical Shia Muslim clerics that govern Iran. This is nothing new for the nation in recent years. What is new is Ahmadinejad's willingness to take these radical clerics' theocratic positions public in places like the United Nations. We are seeing more clearly than ever what is taking place "behind the curtain" in Iran.

IRAN: A TRANSITION TO MILITANCY

Iran is an ancient nation with a history thousands of years old. Religiously speaking, it is Muslim like the other Middle Eastern Arab nations. But ethnically, Iran is not Arab—it is Persian. That is part of the reason for their sense of superiority. Reviewing Iran's modern history will help set the stage for understanding the current crisis.

From the Shah to the Ayatollahs

The Shah of Iran became the head of the government in 1941. But because he grew increasingly friendly toward the West (particularly America and Britain), the religious clerics led an uprising against the Shah, and he was forced to flee with his family in 1979.

A formerly exiled cleric, Ayatollah Khomeini, returned to Iran and assumed control in April of 1979. But in December a new, theocratic constitution had been approved and he was made the Supreme Leader of the Islamic Republic of Iran. Thousands of people loyal to the deposed Shah were executed. Khomeini invoked an ancient Islamic office, the Guardianship of the Religious Jurist, declaring himself to be that revered figure—an heir to the legacy of Muhammad and prior imams. As the Religious Jurist, he "[wielded] absolute authority and sovereignty over the affairs of the entire Islamic nation."[6]

Khomeini died in 1989 and was succeeded by a cleric with a similar name: Ayatollah Ali Khamenei. Khamenei is currently the Supreme Leader of Iran having assumed the Religious Jurist mantel upon Khomeini's death. And his policies and goals are the same: Muslim world domination. In 1989 he told a group of Hezbollah leaders from Lebanon, "Iran's Islamic revolution cannot be confined within its borders, a nation, or ethnic groups. It is in our revolution's interest, and an essential principle, that when we speak of Islamic objectives, we address all the Muslims of the world, and when we speak of the Arrogant West, we address all the oppressors of the world."[7]

President Mahmoud Ahmadinejad was elected to his current political presidency in 2005, running on a hardline religious platform that earned the clerics' support. But not everyone in Iran is happy with him. When he was re-elected in 2009 there were massive demonstrations in Tehran because many believe the elections were rigged. In fact, France, Germany, England, and the United States refused to send the traditional letters of congratulations on his re-election because they believed the elections were a fraud.

From Clerics to a Crisis

Are you getting a sense for why Iran is a calamity waiting to happen? It is the eighteenth largest nation, with the third largest oil supply, run by radical Muslim clerics who believe Iran is the preeminent Arab nation on a mission from God to create chaos in the world, with growing nuclear capability. Israeli Prime Minister Benjamin Netanyahu has said, "You don't want a messianic apocalyptic cult controlling atomic bombs . . ."[8]

In the West, we know very little of the complicated history of the Middle East. Sorting out that history will help us understand the present.

First, religion: Islam is a religion, but Arab is an ethnic group. Almost all Arabs are Muslim, but not all Muslims are Arabs. Iranians are ethnically Persians. They are Persian Muslims, not Arab Muslims. And that creates a tension point between Iran and the other Middle Eastern Muslim nations which are Arabs. Iran believes it is the true keeper of the Muslim faith. That makes her a "bully" in the eyes of the Arab Muslim nations in the region and puts the Arab nations on the defensive. If Iran acquires nuclear weapons, the Arab nations in the region will have to follow suit for their defense. Some analysts think many Arab nations would secretly welcome an attack by Israel on Iran's nuclear facilities. As long as Iran is not nuclear-armed, the other nations don't have to be either.

As far as Israel goes, Iran's posture is not like Hitler's— genocide toward the Jews. Iran is against the Jewish state, not the Jewish people. Ahmadinejad wants the state of Israel out of the Middle East; the Jews can go live somewhere else in the world. Strangely enough, the Jews and the Iranians (Persians) have not always had such an antagonistic relationship. In fact, it was a Persian king several thousand years ago who preserved the Jews from being extinguished as a people.

IRAN: FROM FRIEND TO FOE TO FANATIC

To recount the biblical history:

- 586 B.C., Babylon destroys Jerusalem and takes Jews captive.
- 539 B.C., Babylon is conquered by Medo-Persians and Persia inherits the captive Jews.
- 538 B.C., Cyrus, the Persian king, issues a decree that the Jews should rebuild their temple in Jerusalem (Ezra 1:2-3).

A succession of Persian kings continue to support the return of the Jews to rebuild Jerusalem and its wall. For 130 years the Persian kings provide resources and freedom for the Jews to reestablish themselves in their homeland.

- 486-465 B.C. During the reign of the Persian King Xerxes (Ahasuerus), the restoration of the Jews was almost sabotaged by a hateful Persian official not unlike the modern Ahmadinejad.

A Former Friend of Israel

We pick up that story in the book of Esther. Xerxes' wife disobeyed the king and she was banished from the court—and the king began looking for a new queen. He chose Esther, not knowing she was a Jewess. Esther's cousin, Mordecai, uncovered an assassination plot against the king and the perpetrators were dealt with without Xerxes knowing it was Esther's cousin who saved his life. An official of Xerxes' named Haman developed a hatred for Mordecai because Mordecai would not bow down to him, and Haman convinced Xerxes to have Mordecai and all the Jews in Persia put to death.

Why all the Jews? Why not just Mordecai? Because Haman saw this as an opportunity to settle an old score on behalf of his ancestors. Haman was not a Persian but a descendant of the Amalekites who had attacked Israel when they were moving in to inherit the Promised Land of Canaan. Because of that attack, God commanded that the Amalekites were to be destroyed (Deuteronomy 25:19). Haman, an Amalekite, was descended from Esau while the Jews were descended from Jacob, the line of promise from Abraham through Isaac. Jacob got the blessing by tricking Isaac into giving him, the second-born son, the blessing instead of Esau, the first-born. So when Haman, a descendant of Esau, saw an opportunity to extract vengeance on the descendants of Jacob, the Jews, he took it! And it almost worked.

But Xerxes discovered (Providentially) that it was Mordecai who had uncovered the assassination plot against him and saved his life, and that Haman had planned to kill Mordecai and all the Jews. So the tables were turned—Haman was killed and the Jews were saved at the request of Esther, the Jewish queen of Persia. Jews all over the world today celebrate the deliverance of their ancestors by a Persian king in the feast of Purim (Esther 9:18-26).

That is a *very* condensed version of this wonderful story, the details of which you can read in Esther. But it provides an ironic backdrop to a situation in modern Persia today where the president of Iran is calling for the dissolution, instead of the rebuilding, of the Jewish nation.

A Foe of the International Community

The Muslim religion didn't arrive in modern Iran until a thousand or so years after the time of Esther, so it was not militant Islamism that fueled Haman's hatred of the Jews. The Persian religion of Esther's day was tolerant of Jewish religious beliefs as seen by the Persian kings' support of the reestablishment of Jerusalem. But once Islam arrived in Persia around A.D. 644, things began to change. Islam insisted, over time, that Persians worship Allah, the one true god, and Persia became a Muslim nation, predominantly the Sunni (more moderate) strain. But today, Iran's Muslims are almost all the more radical Shia, including the leaders. The vast majority of Muslims worldwide are more moderate Sunnis.

A Fanatic to Be Watched

In summary, remember these points:

1. Radical Shia Muslims are not tolerant of other faiths.

2. Islam is patient. It took 350 years for Persia to become Muslim, but it happened.

3. Shia Muslims, such as those who rule Iran, have one goal: the implementation of radical Muslim law in every country of the world.

4. Not all Arabs are radical militants; only a minority are.

5. It is futile for the U.S. to negotiate with Iran's leaders. They only want one thing: world domination.

6. Biblical prophecy indicates that an end-times alliance between Russia and Iran to destroy Israel will be thwarted by God near the beginning of the Tribulation (Ezekiel 38-39). God will intervene to save Israel just as He did in the days of Esther and Mordecai.

7. The "Arab Spring" uprisings in Middle East nations that began in early 2011 are a sign of the great instability in the Middle East. We don't know where this will lead, but students of biblical prophecy must pay careful attention to these developments.

The primary conclusion is this: Those who are secure in their relationship with God through Jesus Christ have no reason to fear the rise of Iran or militant Islam or Middle East instability. God's plan and promises, not political developments, are our hope and security. If you do not know Jesus Christ today, I urge you to commit yourself by faith to Him so that you may know nothing can take you out of His hand (John 10:28).

Notes:

1. http://www.un-iran.org/index.php?option=com_content&view=article&id=876:address-by-he-dr-mahmoud-ahmadinejad-president-of-the-islamic-republic-of-iran-before-the-65th-session-of-the-united-nations-general-assembly-new-york-23-september-2010&catid=41:general assembly&Itemid=54, accessed%2027%20September%202010.

2. William Kern, "Ahmadinejad Announces Iranian Plans to 'Administer the Word': Die Welt, Germany," *The Moderate Voice*, 15 December 2009, http://themoderatevoice.com/56031/ahmadinejad-announces-iranian-plans-to-administer-the-world-die-welt-germany/,accessed 18 December 2009.

3. "Ahmadinejad: U.S. Blocking Savior's Return," http://www.upi.com/Top_News/US/2009/12/08/Ahmadinejad-US-blocking-saviors-return/UPI-86901260290829/, accessed 18 December 2009.

4. http://edition.cnn.com/2005/WORLD/meast/10/26/ahmadinejad/, accessed 2-3-11.

5. Dudi Cohen, "Iran Says It Can Destroy Israel in Week," YNET news, 20 May 2010, http://www.ynetnews.com/articles/0,7340,L-3891781,00.html, accessed 29 September 2010.

6. Mohammad Mohaddessin, *Islamic Fundamentalism* (Washington, D.C.: Seven Locks Press, 1993), 17.

7. Cited in Mohammad Mohaddessin, *Islamic Fundamentalism: The New Global Threat* (New Delhi, India: Anmol Publications Pvt. Ltd., 2003) 28.

8. Jeffrey Goldberg, "The Point of No Return," *The Atlantic*, September 2010, http://www.theatlantic.com/magazine/archive/2010/09/the-point-of-no-return/8186, accessed 29 September 2010.

APPLICATION

1. In John 13:35, what did Jesus say should characterize His disciples?

   a. In verse 34, what is the new law that He gave His disciples to live by?

   b. What characteristics do you see in the kind of leadership Jesus described in Matthew 20:25?

   c. What kind of leadership did Jesus say should characterize those in the kingdom of God? (verses 26-28)

   d. How did Jesus exercise servant leadership in His ministry? (See Philippians 2:5-8)

   e. What adjectives would you use to describe someone who leads by serving?

f. Why is servant leadership always more effective than a dictatorial style of leadership?

g. Based on your general knowledge, how would you describe the leadership styles of many of the Arab nations in the Middle East? (Dictatorial? Controlling? Servant?)

h. How do Muslim countries compare with nations like the United States when it comes to religious freedom? Which is more compatible with the human desire to express one's own convictions?

2. Read Luke 14:25-33.

a. Contrast the meaning of "disciple" (a follower) with what the people were doing in verse 25.

b. Why did Jesus seize this opportunity to explain the cost of being His disciple?

c. What are the two measures of discipleship found in verses 26 and 27:

• verse 26: a willingness to_____

• verse 27: a willingness to_____

d. How do these demands of Jesus express the need for commitment and dedication?

e. What principle of discipleship is illustrated in verses 28-30 and verses 31-32?

f. How does Jesus summarize all these teachings about discipleship in verse 33?

g. How does He express this same measure of commitment in John 15:13?

h. Why is the practice of suicide bombers in militant Islam a perversion of the principle of John 15:13?

i. What are some practical ways Jesus expects His disciples to manifest that principle? And what might be the ultimate way?

DID YOU KNOW?

The word "theocracy" is not found in the Bible, but the English word is derived from two New Testament Greek words: *theos* is the word for God, and *kratos* is the word for strength or might. So *theos* plus *kratos* equals theocracy: the ruling might of God. The nation of Israel started out as a pure theocracy with no human rulers as intermediaries between God and the people. There were to be leaders (like Moses and Joshua), priests, prophets, and sages—but no rulers. But the people demanded a king. With a warning about their negative choice, God gave them Saul, and the theocracy became a monarchy—rule by a king—which was a disaster. One day, God will reestablish His theocracy (rule by God) over the earth through the rule of the God-Man, Jesus Christ, as King of kings during the thousand-year millennium.

...WHEN AMERICA WOULD TURN HER BACK ON ISRAEL

Selected Scriptures

In this lesson we will discover the danger in not supporting and blessing the nation of Israel.

OUTLINE

A most unusual promise in Scripture pertains to how one treats the nation of Israel. Those who bless Israel will be blessed while those who curse Israel will be cursed. In recent years, America's support for Israel has wavered, which could have disastrous results for our nation.

   I. **God's Providence in the Story of Israel**

  II. **God's Promise of a Land for Israel**

 III. **God's Punishment of the Enemies of Israel**

 IV. **God's Preservation of America Because of Israel**

  V. **God's Program for the Church and Israel**

 VI. **God's Plan for the Peace of Israel**

On May 19, 2011, President Obama made a speech calling for Israel to return to her pre-1967 borders as a starting place for peace negotiations with the Palestinians. This would mean dividing Israel and Jerusalem again and creating borders for Israel that are indefensible against military attack from all sides.

The president's proposal brought a storm of protest from conservative politicians such as former Speaker of the House Newt Gingrich: "[It was] the most dangerous speech ever made by an American president for the survival of Israel."[1] Former Massachusetts governor Mitt Romney said, "It is disrespectful of Israel for America to dictate negotiating terms to our ally." He also said the president "threw Israel under the bus."[2] Former Minnesota governor Tim Pawlenty said, "The city of Jerusalem must never be re-divided. At this time of upheaval in the Middle East, it's never been more important for America to stand strong for Israel and for a united Jerusalem."[3]

Biblical prophecy and Middle East expert Joel Rosenberg said, "The President made an enormous mistake this week in calling for the land of Israel to be divided and Jerusalem to be divided along pre-1967 borders. This is in direct defiance of the Bible. It won't work and it will bring judgment on the U.S., according to Joel 3. Please pray that the President changes his heart and changes course very soon."[4]

Israel's Prime Minister, Benjamin Netanyahu, responded politely but firmly to the president's proposal by saying Israel would never return to its pre-1967 borders, that it would be up to Palestinian leaders to decide whether they would make alliances with the terrorist organization Hamas or with Israel. In spite of President Obama suggesting a weakening of support for Israel, the prime minister defended Israel's right to sovereignty.

America, under then-President Harry Truman, was one of the first nations to give unqualified support for the establishment of Israel as a nation in 1948. But in recent years that support has been diluted. And in this lesson I want to make the point that Israel is the key to America's survival. You might think the opposite is true —that America is the key to Israel's survival. After all, we are the much larger superpower upon whom Israel depends for certain amounts of foreign aid and military support. On the surface it would make sense to say that America is the key to Israel's survival.

But such is not the case as Genesis 12:3 plainly suggests: "I will bless those who bless you, and I will curse him who curses you;

and in you all the families of the earth shall be blessed." God spoke these words to Abraham concerning his descendants, the nation of Israel. Those who curse Israel will be cursed, and those who bless Israel will be blessed. Given God's perfect track record for promise-keeping, I would not want to be on the "curse" side of that promise. But that is where America is headed as she has weakened her support for Israel in light of the demands and attacks of Israel's militant Arab neighbors.

No nation should take lightly the promise of God in Genesis 12:3 —if for no other reason than self-preservation. And that includes America. Even if American leaders don't fully understand or agree with the Judeo-Christian teachings of the Bible, matching up Genesis 12:3 with the thousands of years of history involving Israel should be convincing enough: Bless Israel and you will be blessed; curse Israel and you will be cursed.

GOD'S PROVIDENCE IN THE STORY OF ISRAEL

God chose a man named Abraham and promised to create a people for Himself through that man and his wife, Sarah (Genesis 12:1-3). Those descendants became God's chosen people (Deuteronomy 7:6-8; Psalm 33:12). God made a promise to Abraham and kept it— and that promise has never been rescinded (Jeremiah 31:35-37). He created a people to demonstrate His loving character to the rest of the world.

And that is the reason for the blessing-cursing promise in Genesis 12:3. God planned to bless the entire world through the nation of Israel (and He has). So to attack God's people is to attack God's plan to bless the world; it is to attack God Himself. That is why any nation's relationship with Israel is a matter of life and death. That is why America's relationship with Israel is the most critical link in the chain that ties us to the blessing of God.

Nations that curse Israel will find themselves in direct confrontation with Israel's God. Nations that bless and support Israel will themselves become the recipients of God's favor and blessing. Tracing the history of nations that have had significant contact with Israel is to trace the Providential hand of God in history.

GOD'S PROMISE OF A LAND FOR ISRAEL

To Abraham (Genesis 13:15, 17; 15:7, 18; 24:7), Isaac (Genesis 26:2-5), and to Jacob and his twelve sons (Exodus 33:1-3) God promised a homeland. It was the land of Canaan when Abraham first arrived there and became the "land of promise" (Hebrews 11:9), or Promised Land (Deuteronomy 19:8), when the Hebrew slaves came out of Egypt to inherit it. Israel lived in the land and became powerful under kings David and Solomon, but was taken into captivity in Assyria and Babylon. A portion of the people returned to the land to rebuild Jerusalem and the temple; but in A.D. 70 the Roman army destroyed Jerusalem again. The Jews entered the great Diaspora, scattered across the face of the earth.

Partially after World War I, and in earnest following World War II, Jews began returning to their homeland. Tensions with Arabs were momentarily relieved when the United Nations agreed to Israel's statehood in 1948. The argument is frequently made that the Jews came in and displaced the Arabs from their lands. But the truth is that the land belongs to God, and God gave it to the Jews thousands of years ago as an "inheritance forever" (Joshua 14:9).

Yes, Israel was absent from the land from A.D. 70 to 1948—by God's design (Romans 11:11-32). But that changes nothing. Just because politics and legalities are more complicated in the modern era does not change the ancient truth that Israel's land is hers by assignment from God (Acts 17:26). Israel is still the apple of God's eye (Deuteronomy 32:10), and woe to any nation, including the Unites States, who fails to recognize that fact.

The first book I ever wrote, *Before It's Too Late* (1975), had a whole chapter devoted to how God has blessed America as a result of America welcoming and supporting the Jewish people. History is littered with the ruins of other nations that cursed Israel and who were themselves destroyed. The question for America is whether we will learn from history or not.

GOD'S PUNISHMENT OF THE ENEMIES OF ISRAEL

Zechariah 2:8 says that "he who touches [Israel] touches the apple of His eye." Later in chapter nine Zechariah provides a roll call of nations that would come under God's judgment for their treatment of Israel—all of which have vanished from history. And in Zechariah 9:8 God says, "I will set up camp in my home country and defend it against invaders. Nobody is going to hurt my people ever again. I'm keeping my eye on them" (*The Message*).

More nations could be added to the list—nations that either suffered significantly or disappeared. In the modern era the most pointed example is Germany which was decimated by Allied armies in World War II following the Jewish Holocaust. In all these cases, ancient and modern, nations lifted their hand against the Jews and suffered for it.

Great Britain is another modern example to which we in America can relate. Once the most powerful nation in the world (nineteenth century), Britain was given responsibility for much of the Middle East following World War I and was supportive of "the establishment in Palestine of a national home for the Jewish people" (Balfour Declaration, 1917). But between 1917 and 1948, when Britain's oversight ended and the United Nations partitioned Palestine into two areas, one Palestinian and the other Jewish, England gradually withdrew her support for Israel. England even supported the Palestinians with arms in their ongoing conflicts with Israel, seemingly turning her back and breaking the promise she made in 1917. After World War I they actually stopped Jewish immigration into Palestine from Europe, which probably resulted in the deaths of many Jews during the Holocaust.

When the United Nations voted on partitioning Palestine in 1947, England abstained from voting; she wouldn't support Israel's efforts to hold on to her land. England assumed that the Arabs would conquer the Jews and drive them out of the land and that would be the end of the problem. But neither England nor the Palestinians counted on the Jews' ability to defend themselves and their land. Israel won war after war with the Arab nations that surrounded her and won back the land she holds today.

But here is the point for America: I believe you can chart the decline of Great Britain as the world's superpower from the years in which she turned her back on the Jews in their attempt to reestablish themselves in their homeland. What happened to Great Britain? Almost exactly parallel to her walking away from her promises to Israel, Great Britain has descended down a long slope of insignificance and no longer is even considered among the major powers of the world.

GOD'S PRESERVATION OF AMERICA BECAUSE OF ISRAEL

From the beginning of this nation, America has welcomed the Jews. Twenty-three Jewish immigrants arrived in New Amsterdam (New York City) in 1654, and by the early 1700s it is estimated there were 250 Jews living in the colonies.[5] In fact, a Jewish businessman name Haym Solomon played a pivotal role in financing General George Washington's military campaigns in the Revolutionary War.[6]

I've already mentioned the fact that President Truman, in 1948, openly declared America's support for the founding of the new nation of Israel—in spite of the strident opposition of his top advisors. Harry Truman had been raised reading the Bible and knew enough to know that God had a plan for Israel and that he wasn't going to stand in the way. And many other American presidents have stood with Israel.

But something is changing. And I fear what happened to England may be about to happen to America. A 2010 survey showed that 52 percent of Americans believe that our current president (Obama) is less friendly to Israel than any former administration.[7] Recent presidents—the first president Bush, Jimmy Carter, Bill Clinton—have promoted the "land for peace" initiatives, trying to get Israel to give up her land for a promise of peace from Arabs. And now oil has entered the equation—oil that America desperately needs from oil-producing Arab states.

In his first foreign policy trip in June, 2009, President Obama told an Arab audience in Cairo that the Palestinian people have suffered for 60 years (the time since Israel became a state in 1948) as refugees dislocated from their own land. This speech was not a strong statement of support for Israel. Rather it was a political speech to lay groundwork for mutual concessions.[8] For some reason, it is always Israel being asked to give up her homeland.

With Great Britain no longer "great," America's leaders must not go down the same path. America has been a great nation because of God's blessing. But God does not bless nations that do not bless His chosen people.

God's Program for the Church and Israel

Sadly, many Christians today are contributing indirectly to America's lack of loyalty to Israel by subscribing to something called Replacement Theology. This theological view holds that the modern state of Israel has no biblical relevance; that Israel of the Old Testament has been replaced by the Church of the New Testament; that unfulfilled Old Testament prophecies have been fulfilled spiritually in the Church through Jesus Christ.

Replacement Theology raises more questions than it provides answers. When we don't interpret the clear teachings of the Bible literally it becomes anyone's guess as to what verses mean. Just because there is not a clear spiritual turning of Israel to her Messiah doesn't mean that God is not at work in His chosen people. Paul says in Romans 11:26-27 that He will fulfill His covenant with them one day when He takes away their sins, when He turns away "ungodliness from Jacob." The nation has only been back in her homeland since 1948! Compared to wandering the earth since A. D. 70, this is a very recent movement—baby steps in the beginning of Israel's ultimate turning to the Lord: "And so all Israel will be saved" (Romans 11:26).

Israel's status before God has not changed; she has not been replaced by the Church. Jeremiah 31:35-37 says the foundations of the universe would have to be shaken before that would happen.

GOD'S PLAN FOR THE PEACE OF ISRAEL

I want my country to be blessed by God because of our loyal support for God's chosen people. And there are two things I can do to help that happen.

First, I can use all the means at my disposal to influence those who establish national policies in Washington, D. C. We can vote, write letters, and call our senators and representatives concerning legislation that affects Israel. The Declaration of Independence says that governments should "[derive] their just powers from the consent of the governed." And we are the governed who have a duty to influence our government.

Second, we can "pray for the peace of Jerusalem" (Psalm 122:6) and for our leaders (1 Timothy 2:1-4). If Christians around the world would pray for the safety and sovereignty of the state of Israel against the attacks of all her enemies, who knows what kind of breakthrough might occur?

I'm often asked about America's role in the future since we seem not to be mentioned anywhere in biblical prophecy. My great fear is that America might become an insignificant part of the future of planet earth because of God's withheld blessing based on our failure to bless His chosen people. May that not be so! May we continue to support the apple of God's eye so she may continue her calling as a blessing to all the nations of the earth.

Notes:

1. Philip Elliott, "Romney: Obama 'threw Israel under the bus,'" May 19, 2011, Associated Press. http://hosted2.ap.org/APDEFAULT/login/Article_2011-05-19-Obama-Mideast--Republicans/id-c2010ab08371464ba02f82363d8df781, accessed 6-2-11.

2. Ibid.

3. Ibid.

4. Joel C. Rosenberg, "Warning to the Nations: Don't Divide the Land of Israel," *Joel C. Rosenberg's Blog: Tracking events and trends in Israel, Russia and the epicenter*, 19 May 2011, http://flashtrafficblog.wordpress.com/, accessed 22 May 2011.

5. Jerry Klinger, "The Canary in the Coal Mine? American Jewry 1654-1770," *The Jewish Magazine*, http://www.jewishmag.com/79mag/usahistory2/usahistory2.htm, accessed 10 May 2011.

6. http://en.wikipedia.org/wiki/Hayim_solomon, accessed 5 May 2011.

7. McLaughlin & Associates, "National Survey October 5, 2010," http://www.committeeforisrael.com/wp-content/uploads/2010/10/ECI-National-Poll-October.pdf, accessed 12 October 2010.

8. "Text: Obama's Speech in Cairo," *The New York Times*, 4 June 2009, http://www.nytimes.com/2009/06/04/us/politics/04obama.text.html?pagewanted=1&adxnnlx=1304006424-qJNyzY0YUQPF6d7kZqJW7w, accessed 5 May 2011.

APPLICATION

1. Read Deuteronomy 7:6-8.

   a. What is the setting of these words? (See Deuteronomy 1:1-5.)

   b. After developing for more than 400 years, Israel is now a large nation. Why are the words of Moses in 7:6-8 appropriate at this point?

   c. Describe the way God looked at the people of Israel. (verse 6)

   d. What does Moses eliminate as the reason for God choosing Israel? (verse 7)

   e. What does "least of all peoples" mean? (How many people did God start with? [Genesis 12:1] What was their condition when God called them out of Egypt?)

f. What two reasons for Israel's uniqueness does Moses give? (verse 8)

1) Because He_____you.

2) Because of the_____He made to their forefathers.

2. Read 1 Peter 2:9-10.

a. How does Peter apply the "chosen people" terminology to the Church? (verse 9)

b. How do we know the Church is not the same as Israel? (verse 10a) (How long had Israel been the people of God? How long has the Church been the people of God?)

c. What did we receive that allowed us to be included among the people of God? (verse 10b)

d. In light of that gift, what does Paul say we should do? (Romans 12:1)

3. Read Jeremiah 31:35-37.

a. What does God say would cause Israel to cease being a nation before Him forever? (verses 35-36)

b. What would cause God to cast off the seed of Israel? (verse 37)

c. Have any of these conditions been met? If not, what does that say about the current status of Israel as a nation before God?

4. What effect will the inclusion of the Gentiles into God's blessing have on Israel? (Romans 11:11)

a. What imagery does Paul use to describe the inclusion of Gentiles? (Romans 11:17-21)

b. What will eventually happen to Israel? (Romans 11:23, 26)

DID YOU KNOW?

The phrase "apple of your [or His] eye" occurs four times in the Old Testament. Twice it refers to Israel as the apple of God's eye; once to the psalmist as the apple of God's eye; and once to God's law. It is obviously a term of endearment or of value. But the Hebrew phrase is literally translated, "the little man of your eye." The reference is to the pupil of the eye in which a tiny reflection may be found of the person staring into one's face. Worth is implied in more than one way: The little man in God's eye is safe in the depths of His being; or the pupil—representing eyesight itself—is of inestimable value. The loss of eyesight was a great reproach in the ancient world (Numbers 16:14; Judges 16:21).

...WHEN CHANGING YOUR MIND COULD SAVE YOUR LIFE

Romans 12:1-2

In this lesson we learn how not to be conformed to the standards and values of this world.

OUTLINE

There is no neutral ground in this world. We are either being conformed to the world or transformed into the image of Christ by the renewing of our mind. But this transformation doesn't happen automatically. It requires a decision, determination, and daily discipline.

I. **A Radical Decision**
   A. It's Crucial
   B. It's Comprehensive
   C. It's Costly
   D. It's Creative
   E. It's Credible

II. **A Rational Determination**
   A. Being Conformed
   B. Being Transformed

III. **A Rigorous Discipline**
   A. Two Agents: The Holy Spirit and the Word of God
   B. Two Actions: Outside-In and Inside-Out

IV. **A Routine Demonstration**
   A. You Will Learn the Will of God
   B. You Will Live the Will of God
   C. You Will Love the Will of God

The preceding nine chapters in this study guide have laid out, often in shocking terms, developments that are relatively new in our society. We've looked at changes in the attitude of atheists, at spiritual warfare, the way Jesus is profaned, how marriage is becoming optional, at the loss of our moral compass, the marginalization of the Bible, the growing irrelevancy of the Church, the rise of Iran as a threat to world stability, and America's changing posture toward Israel.

That is a lot of change to absorb in one lifetime—and I fear the changes are going to keep coming. Therefore, we have to ask ourselves, "How do we stand firm under the onslaught of so many significant changes happening around us?" The world may be changing, but we want to stand firm and not be moved off of our foundation. The world's values may be changing (and even those of some Christians), but we want to keep our core biblical values and beliefs in place. Here's why this is such an important issue: There is no middle ground. Because the culture is changing negatively, we will change with it if we are not actively engaged in *not changing*.

But that is not enough. *Not changing* is the equivalent of resting on our laurels, relying on what we learned last year to get us through next year. We have to be maturing faster than the culture is "immaturing." We have to be continually deepening our faith and our core kingdom values if we are going to be the salt and light God expects us to be in this world.

And that is the focus of this chapter. We're going to learn to do what the apostle Paul advised the Church in Rome to do when they were living in a similar, secular society: *Resist* being transformed by the *world* by *renewing* our mind with the *Word*. Paul wrote in Romans 12:1-2,

> I beseech you therefore, brethren, by the mercies of God, that you present your bodies a living sacrifice, holy, acceptable to God, which is your reasonable service. And do not be conformed to this world, but be transformed by the renewing of your mind, that you may prove what is that good and acceptable and perfect will of God.

This is the clearest biblical admonition I know as a long-term defense against being transformed by the world around us.

A RADICAL DECISION

There are five dimensions to the importance of the decision to become a living sacrifice and renew our mind.

It's Crucial

The key word from Paul in verse 1 is "beseech." It's a strong word, akin to "beg." This is an important matter Paul is writing about, and they have a crucial decision to make. And he is begging them to make it. And the basis for Paul's request is the "mercies of God." In the final verses of chapter 11 Paul mentions God's mercy four times and now says, "by the mercies of God," or "in view of God's mercy" (NIV). He is saying, "Based on the mercy God has shown you, what I'm about to ask you to do is perfectly reasonable." Paul's thinking here parallels that of the apostle John: "We love Him because He first loved us" (1 John 4:19).

I recall hearing Dr. D. James Kennedy years ago on the radio saying, "Every believer in Christ should live the rest of his life as a 'P.S.: I love You' to God." And he was right. In light of what He has done for us, how could we do less?

It's Comprehensive

The word "present" in verse 1 is reminiscent of the Old Testament sacrifices where Israelites would bring an animal or part of their harvest and "present" it to the Lord. Paul is encouraging us to do the same—to present ourselves to God as a living sacrifice. And, of course, "body" doesn't refer just to skin and bones, our physical self. It refers to the totality of who we are: "Lord, the world is getting more unpredictable every year. I can't know what the world is going to do next, but I can entrust my entire life to You—everything I am and everything I have I offer to You as a living sacrifice." It's the same idea Paul expressed in Romans 6:13: "present yourselves [your 'members'—all parts of you] to God . . ."

I remember going to church summer camps as a young person and making a "total commitment" to Christ on the last night of camp. And the next summer, I would make another commitment since I knew I hadn't done a good job of trusting the Lord the previous 12 months. That's okay—God looks at our heart and honors the desire of people old and young to commit themselves totally to Him. It's the only way to make sense out of the world in which we live.

It's Costly

This decision is not inexpensive! In fact, just like Jesus' decision to sacrifice Himself on the cross, it will cost you all that you are every day for the rest of your life. Why? Because you are becoming a "living sacrifice." Again, like Jesus died to Himself every day to do the will of the Father (John 5:31), so we must die daily and live unto God. Someone has said that the problem with living sacrifices is that they keep crawling off the altar! The price will be great, but the rewards greater.

It's Creative

I often have people ask me how they can know the will of God for their life. It's much easier than they think: The will of God is the Word of God. I know—we all want to know specifics about the future. But that's not where we begin. We begin by obeying all the will of God found in Scripture—that will of God that is the same for everyone—and trust God to show us the details as we are walking in obedience to Him. It's like my father told me as a boy growing up: "David, get the car moving. It's much easier to steer a moving car than one that is stopped."

It's Credible

There is nothing unreasonable about what Paul is asking us to do. In fact, he says presenting ourselves to God as a living sacrifice is our "reasonable service." The word "reasonable" in Greek is the word on which our word "logical" is based. What we're doing is logical; it is reasonable; it is credible.

Why is giving yourself wholeheartedly to God reasonable? Because we need His help and strength to navigate the dangerous waters we go through daily in our world. We need someone bigger than us, someone who knows the future, someone who has a plan that will see us through. Not to mention, it is reasonable in light of what He has already done for us.

Pastor John MacArthur has written,

True worship does not consist of elaborate and impressive prayers, intricate liturgy, stained glass windows, lighted candles, flowing robes, incense, and classical sacred music. It does not require great talent, skill, or leadership ability. Many of these things can be a part of the outward worship, but they are acceptable to God only in the heart and mind of the worshipper who is focused on Him. The only spiritual service of worship that honors and pleases God is the sincere, loving, thoughtful, heartfelt devotion and praise of His children.[1]

A RATIONAL DETERMINATION

Not only is this a radical decision we have to make, it is also a rational determination that involves two issues: conformation and transformation.

Being Conformed

Step one is to offer yourself as a living sacrifice to God which is preparatory to the second step: being transformed by the renewing of your mind: "And do not be conformed to this world, but be transformed by the renewing of your mind . . ." (verse 2).

I said earlier there is no neutral ground. We are continually being conformed or transformed—conformed to the shape of the world around us or transformed by the renewing of our mind. Pressure to conform to the world is relentless through our daily exposure to it—now more than ever through the always-on media. I can remember as a child that very little television programming was tolerated in our home, especially commercials for products that were not edifying. Yet today, television is part of the average family's life. We have grown used to it; we tolerate it even when we know it isn't edifying.

One of my sons attended two different universities to play college football, and in both locations came to realize he was about the only Christian on the team. He would often tell me about the pressure he felt to conform to behavioral standards he wasn't comfortable with as a Christian. We finally decided that the best way to resist the pressures to conform was to be outspoken about his faith. When he did, the other players learned to leave him alone; they learned he wasn't going to conform and they backed off. The same is true for us—the best way to resist conformity is by continually being proactive about our faith.

Conformity is pressure from the outside, in. Instead of being conformed, we need to be transformed from the inside, out.

Being Transformed

The Greek word for transformed is the word from which we get "metamorphosis"—that process inside a cocoon that turns a caterpillar into a butterfly. It happens from the inside out.

The best way to be transformed from the inside out is described by Paul: "by the renewing of your mind." Because we are as we think, the more we renew our mind with the truth of God's Word, the more we will be transformed from the inside out. If we are continually being transformed, then the world cannot conform us to its image.

Pastor Andy Stanley has written, "Men and women, you can spend the rest of your lives making promises, filling out commitment cards, talking to counselors, but Paul's words are very clear. Unless you renew your mind, you won't be transformed. Things will stay pretty much the way that they are."[2]

A Rigorous Discipline

We've identified a radical decision and a rational determination not to be conformed to the world. But there must also be a rigorous discipline to allow those decisions to be sustained into the future: "by the renewing of your mind . . ."

The idea behind renewal is renovation. Anyone who has ever renovated a house knows the process: out with the old, in with the new. And it is the same with the mind. We must replace the world's way of thinking with God's way; replace the world's version of "truth" with God's true truth. I have spent my entire adult life dedicated to one purpose: spreading the Word of God. Why would I do that? Because it is the truth that will set mankind free from the grip of the world, sin, and the devil (John 8:32). If you are to renew your mind, you must fill your mind with God's truth so you can look at what is happening in the world the same way God does.

Two Agents: The Holy Spirit and The Word of God

Ephesians 4:23 talks about renewing "the spirit of your mind." Titus 3:5 talks about the renewing ministry of the Holy Spirit. The same two realities that save us—the Word and the Holy Spirit— also renew us and transform us. The more of the Word you have in your mind, the more the Holy Spirit can use it to help you think like God thinks, which is what we need in the day in which we are living.

Two Actions: Outside-In and Inside-Out

The Word of God comes into our life from the outside. Once it is inside of us, it comes out through us, revealing to the world a transformed person. We become the "new creation" Paul wrote about in 2 Corinthians 5:17.

Again, remember: There is no middle ground. This is a daily, rigorous discipline. Someone said to me not long ago that one of the problems with the Christian life is that it's so daily. And he was right! The pressure of the world is daily, so our response must be daily as well. This cannot be a Sunday-only discipline. That is not enough to resist the conforming pressure of the world.

A Routine Demonstration

Decision, determination, and discipline will result in a routine demonstration of a life consistent with the kingdom of God—not the kingdom of this world. We will "prove [demonstrate] what is that good and acceptable and perfect will of God."

You Will Learn the Will of God

The more the Word of God shapes our life from the inside out, the deeper sense we get of God's particular will for our life. This only happens over time—that's the way it has worked out in my own life. In John 7:17, Jesus spoke about a willingness to know and do God's will; and with that willingness comes revelation from God about what that will is.

Many Christians fear giving up their life to the Lord as a living sacrifice for fear He will call them to do something they don't want to do. But as the Word conforms our will to God's will over time, we find ourselves eager to demonstrate God's presence in our life by obeying His will.

You Will Live the Will of God

It's true in all areas of life: The more we learn, the more we live out what we are learning. And it's true spiritually as well. Many Christians are not excited about living for God because they don't know God and His Word well enough. But we have to begin at the beginning. Learning leads to living out the will of God. And the more we live, the more excited we are about learning. God is an inexhaustible reservoir of surprises and awakenings if we will only trust Him by committing ourselves to Him as living sacrifices.

You Will Love the Will of God

Who wouldn't love a life that is "good and acceptable and perfect"? Our life on earth will never be perfect, but the will of God always will be. And the more our life conforms to God's will, the more we will love the will of God as it is worked out through us.

If you have never paused and said, "Lord, I present myself to You as a living sacrifice," I encourage you to do so today. As the Word begins to renew your mind from the inside out, you will be able to stand firm against the ever-changing world in which we live.

Notes:

1. John MacArthur, *The MacArthur New Testament Commentary - Romans 1-8* (Chicago: Moody Press, 1991) 148.

2. Andy Stanley, *Louder Than Words* (Colorado Springs, CO: Multnomah Brooks, 2004), 89.

APPLICATION

1. Romans 8:28-29.

   a. Contrast the use of the word "conformed" in Romans 8:29 with how it is used in Romans 12:2. What two opposite directions do they present?

   b. Instead of conformity to the world, to what are Christians going to be ultimately conformed? (verse 29)

   c. Who is to be the Christian's elder brother in spiritual terms? (verse 29)

   d. How does knowledge of God's plan for conformation add extra understanding to the well-known verse 28?

   e. What is the "purpose" to which Christians are being called? (verses 28-29)

f. How can events in the world around us contribute to being conformed to the image of Christ? (See Romans 5:3-5.)

g. How has one (or more) of the changes described in chapters 1-9 served to strengthen your faith in recent weeks or months?

2. Read 2 Timothy 3:14-17.

a. How does the idea of "continuing in" reinforce the notion of the Christian life being "so daily," the need for daily discipline? (verse 14)

b. What benefit does Paul ascribe to the "Holy Scriptures" in verse 15? How can you apply that idea ("wise for salvation") to living in a world that is changing for the worse?

c. In what four ways is the Word of God profitable? (verse 16)

d. How can those four benefits apply when living in a world that is changing for the worse?

e. What is the ultimate benefit of the Word of God? (verse 17) How does "every" provide encouragement when faced with an uncertain future in this world?

3. How does Ephesians 4:20-24 parallel the idea of Romans 12:1-2?

a. What are some ways you can incorporate Scripture into your life to enhance the renewing of "the spirit of your mind"? (verse 22-24)

b. What "normal" cultural activities are counterproductive to renewing "the spirit of your mind"? (verse 22)

c. How does our world work against the goal of "true righteousness and holiness"? (verse 24) And what is Paul's long-term solution? (Romans 12:2)

DID YOU KNOW?

Romans 12:1-2 is one of the most well-known passages in the Bible. Within Romans it serves as a bridge between the two "halves" of the book: chapters 1-11 (theology) and 12-16 (application). And the key word in that bridge is the first word in Romans 12:1: "Therefore" (NIV). The most famous translation of Romans 12:1-2 is found in the paraphrase of the New Testament by the Anglican clergyman, J. B. Phillips (1906-1982), *The New Testament in Modern English*: "With eyes wide open to the mercies of God, I beg you, my brothers, as an act of intelligent worship, to give him your bodies, as a living sacrifice, consecrated to him and acceptable by him. Don't let the world around you squeeze you into its own mould, but let God re-mould your minds from within, so that you may prove in practice that the plan of God for you is good, meets all his demands and moves towards the goal of true maturity."

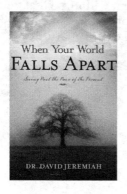

Looking for the Savior
A Study of the Thessalonian Epistles
(two volume study guide set)

Apostle Paul wrote two letters to the new Christians in Thessalonica to help them keep the faith, remain holy, and weather the persecution from those around them. They had a strong start spiritually, and Paul wanted them to continue that way. *Looking for the Savior*, the study of First and Second Thessalonians, will help you strengthen your own faith and learn to encourage young believers who are just starting on their faith journey.

Claiming Faith, Finding Freedom
The Study of Galatians
(two volume study guide set)

In *Claiming Faith, Finding Freedom*, Dr. David Jeremiah takes us on a verse-by-verse journey into Paul's incredible letter to that early church. Paul's argument for justification by faith alone and the supremacy of Christ over the law is as relevant and real today as it was two thousand years ago. Discover once again the freedom we have in Christ through this important study of the Book of Galatians.

Each of these resources was created from a teaching series by Dr. David Jeremiah. Additional resources are available at www.DavidJeremiah.org

For pricing information and ordering, contact us at

with Dr. David Jeremiah

P.O. Box 3838
San Diego, CA 92163
(800) 947-1993
www.DavidJeremiah.org

STAY CONNECTED
TO DR. DAVID JEREMIAH

Take advantage of two great ways to let Dr. David Jeremiah give you spiritual direction every day! Both are absolutely FREE.

Turning Points Magazine and Devotional

Receive Dr. David Jeremiah's monthly magazine, *Turning Points* each month:

- Monthly study focus
- 48 pages of life-changing reading
- Relevant articles
- Special features
- Humor section
- Family section
- Daily devotional readings for each day of the month
- Bible study resource offers
- Live event schedule
- Radio & television information

Your Daily Turning Point E-Devotional

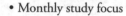

Start your day off right! Find words of inspiration and spiritual motivation waiting for you on your computer every morning! You can receive a daily e-devotion communication from Dr. David Jeremiah that will strengthen your walk with God and encourage you to live the authentic Christian life.

There are two easy ways to sign up for these free resources from Turning Point. Visit us online at www.DavidJeremiah.org and select "Subscribe to Daily Devotional by Email" or visit the home page and find Daily Devotional to subscribe to your monthly copy of *Turning Points*.